Change Your Words, Change Your World

Change Your Words, Change Your World

ANDREA GARDNER

INSIGHTS

First published and distributed in the United Kingdom by:
Hay House UK Ltd, 292B Kensal Rd, London W10 5BE. Tel.: (44) 20 8962 1230;
Fax: (44) 20 8962 1239. www.hayhouse.co.uk

Published and distributed in the United States of America by:
Hay House, Inc., PO Box 5100, Carlsbad, CA 92018-5100. Tel.: (1) 760 431 7695
or (800) 654 5126; Fax: (1) 760 431 6948 or (800) 650 5115. www.hayhouse.com

Published and distributed in Australia by:
Hay House Australia Ltd, 18/36 Ralph St, Alexandria NSW 2015. Tel.: (61) 2 9669 4299;
Fax: (61) 2 9669 4144. www.hayhouse.com.au

Published and distributed in the Republic of South Africa by:
Hay House SA (Pty), Ltd, PO Box 990, Witkoppen 2068. Tel./Fax: (27) 11 467 8904.
www.hayhouse.co.za

Published and distributed in India by:
Hay House Publishers India, Muskaan Complex, Plot No.3, B-2, Vasant Kunj, New Delhi –
110 070. Tel.: (91) 11 4176 1620; Fax: (91) 11 4176 1630. www.hayhouse.co.in

Distributed in Canada by:
Raincoast, 9050 Shaughnessy St, Vancouver, BC V6P 6E5. Tel.: (1) 604 323 7100;
Fax: (1) 604 323 2600

The author of this book does not dispense medical advice or prescribe the use of any technique
as a form of treatment for physical or medical problems without the advice of a physician, either
directly or indirectly. The intent of the author is only to offer information of a general nature
to help you in your quest for emotional and spiritual wellbeing. In the event you use any of
the information in this book for yourself, which is your constitutional right, the author and the
publisher assume no responsibility for your actions.

A catalogue record for this book is available from the British Library.

ISBN 978-1-84850-808-8

Printed and bound in Great Britain.

For Seth, Charlotte and Sophie with love.

CONTENTS

FOREWORD

THE POWER OF WORDS

Words can change your brain, and the right words spoken in the right way can generate mutual rapport with others. The right words can enable cooperation, while the wrong words can generate conflict in less than a second. And if you continue to communicate with negativity, even for a few minutes, you may actually damage your brain. That's what our latest neuroscientific research has found.

Words generate thoughts, and thoughts change the way you perceive the world. Positive thoughts generate feelings of peacefulness and serenity, whereas negative thoughts generate anxiety, fear and doubt. Recent studies have even shown that gazing at a list of positive words makes you feel better but a list of negative words makes you feel worse. Thus if you want to achieve any degree of success in the world – be it in business or in love – you have to choose the right words that will inspire your brain to take positive actions in the world.

But here's the problem: most of our thoughts – and the words that comprise them – are unconscious, and thus we're rarely aware of how the negative ones are interfering with our ability to achieve our goals. If we want to improve our lives and the world in which we live, we must learn to listen to the inner stories, which are constantly spinning in our minds and transform the negativity into life-affirming words.

Andrea calls this the 'incessant internal dialogue', and research shows that this inner speech begins in the first two years of life. By the age of ten it becomes unconscious, but the inner noise continues to shape nearly everything we say and feel and do.

If we don't like the stories we hear, all we have to do is rewrite our inner script, bringing in words of optimism. We can choose words that empower us to take action, we can choose arbitrarily to suppress words that undermine our confidence, and if we keep a list of our positive words and gratitude, our self-esteem and satisfaction with life will soar.

Changing our inner speech

Internal dialogues are constantly racing through our mind at spectacular speeds, and this causes us to talk faster when conversing with others. But if we deliberately slow down our speech, we not only increase the listener's comprehension, we also lower physical tension and stress in both the listener and ourselves. As we relax into our positive words and dialogue, we also interrupt the mechanisms that cause misunderstandings and conflict.

When you speak *very* slowly, and *very* briefly, you'll begin to hear your own inner speech telling you what you should and should not do. Sometimes it sounds like a nasty parent, and sometimes it just sounds crazy, but that's the nature of everyday consciousness, and it keeps you so caught up inside yourself that it becomes virtually impossible to connect with what anyone else is saying.

By slowing down your inner and outer speech, you can begin to choose your words more wisely. Each one will take on more power, compassion, and meaning, and the process will begin to stimulate inspirational thoughts in the listener's brain. In fact, the other person's brain will begin to mirror what you're feeling. It's a process we call 'neural resonance' and it's the most effective way to build mutual understanding and trust. You can even use silence to increase the power of your words, and thus inspire others to become more conscious.

The power of silence

Andrea's story will inspire you, but the inspiration comes from your imagination, not from the actual words in this book. Words are just words, symbols that are unique to every person on this planet. Take, for example, the word 'love'. We all know what it means, and yet if you ask someone to define it, everyone comes up with something different. I'll give you a personal example. I really *love* chocolate. I love deep conversations, I love science, and I really love my family. But each of these 'loves' is fundamentally different. That difference is reflected in the tone of the voice, and in the memories that hold on to those images and feelings of love.

In fact, words are the least important part of the communication process. Andrea and her husband Seth captured this astonishing fact in a film, which runs for less than 90 seconds. It is the foundation on which this book is based, and it's one of the most moving videos I've ever seen. It's so powerful that I now use it in every class I teach. If you haven't seen this film, called *The Power of Words*, go to YouTube right now using this link: http://www.youtube.com/watch?v=Hzgzim5m7oU

I've watched it over and over, and each time it brings tears to my eyes. It will touch the same emotional chords in you, bringing up sadness and joy, and if I were to scan your brain while watching it, it would stimulate some of the most important neural circuits involved with social awareness and compassion.

How is that possible? How can a few words, 'spoken' in silence, move your heart, your brain, and your soul? The answer to that question will be found in the pages of this book, but you'll have to surrender yourself to the hidden images that are evoked in your own imagination.

In the book Andrea shares her journey, where she finds herself nearly penniless, struggling to survive. But she is not filled with worry, fear, or doubt. Instead, she holds onto a sacred inner dream, a dream filled with hope and vibrant faith. Her story and her words will change your brain and change your life. And you can do the same. You can embrace your own story and your own words and live them from your heart. When you do so, you'll bring more joy and peace into the world as together we travel down this marvellous path of life.

Thank you, Andrea, for changing my world with your words!

Mark Robert Waldman
Adjunct Faculty, Loyola Marymount University, Los Angeles, and author of *Words Can Change Your Brain: 12 Strategies to Build Trust, Resolve Conflicts, and Increase Intimacy*

INTRODUCTION

INNER CONVERSATIONS

....

'The world we see that seems so insane is the result of a belief system that is not working. To perceive the world differently, we must be willing to change our belief system, let the past slip away, expand our sense of now, and dissolve the fear in our minds.'

William James

....

I always chuckle to myself at airports, waiting to board a flight.

'Do you have any baggage to check in please?'

Oh yes, plenty.

'And did you pack your baggage yourself?'

Well, other people sometimes gave me stuff to carry around for them but it was me who decided what would stay.

'Could anyone have tampered with your baggage?'

I'd like to see them try!

I happily wave off my case, feeling free and adventurous for a few hours. But when I land in another country, I discover it has followed me, faithful and familiar. Half of me is relieved, while the other half knows the bondage of recognition and regrets what its retrieval from the circular trundle means. But I pick it up because it's mine.

And so it is with personal baggage. It might be uncomfortable to lug around with us but we wouldn't know who we were without it. Yet let's face it, half the time we don't even know what we've packed!

I believe that when troubles show up in our lives it's a call to action: an opportunity to go within to the 'heart of the matter' and listen to our inner wisdom. Perhaps a chance to open up that baggage, take a good look and clear out anything that no longer serves a positive purpose in our lives. The tools we need are the perceptions we hold, the thoughts we think and the words we use.

The origins of beliefs

Psychologists tell us that most of our beliefs are formed between the ages of three and 12. This is when our view of the world and how it works becomes deeply embedded in our brains. It is also the time when we are most receptive and least discerning, and so it's hoped that the adults we depend on during that phase have our best interests at heart. Even in 'stable' family environments where our parents are doing their level best, an adult might still be carrying around inherited negative belief systems, which they've never thought to question or maybe aren't even aware of. It's easy to see how patterns get repeated – our teachers can't teach us what they haven't yet learned themselves.

We are constantly telling ourselves internal stories. In his *Magical Mind, Magical Body* series Deepak Chopra provides us with a startling fact: we have up to 50,000 thoughts every day and 98 per cent of those thoughts are the same as yesterday. So if we're walking around with a collection of beliefs, which were mostly formed from others' experiences and passed onto us as children, then repeating those thoughts pretty much verbatim each day, is it any wonder that our lives keep showing up how we expect them to? And when change does come along we generally tend to try and wrestle it to the floor.

But what are we afraid of? Nothing genuinely stays the same. Realistically each of our thoughts and every one of our cells has the potential for change every second of every day. Let's take our perception of our bodies, for example. Our physical bodies are a collection of all our ideas about them. If we change our words, we can change our world. This means that if we change our inner stories and ideas about ourselves, we can also change our bodies.

When we feel low or unwell, someone might ask us 'What's the matter?'

We speak of 'mind over matter' when we want to overcome a physical barrier or condition. Matter is defined as the stuff that things are made of and it consists of chemical substances. Quantum physics and neuroscience will tell you that matter is influenced by energy, and that energy can be thought patterns and emotions, as well as physical energy. Therefore if the quality of our thoughts and emotions can influence our physical body, if we are consciously directing and shaping those thoughts, it follows that we can consciously create the stuff around and inside us.

Listen to your body

Imbalances manifest on several different levels before they become physical, which is why energy rebalancing techniques such as Reiki and faith healing can work. Physical matter is the densest of our energy fields and it can take a lot of effort to remove something from this level if we haven't cleared the emotional and spiritual disequilibrium too. If we don't get to the root cause of a medical/physical problem by reaching the 'heart of the matter', we are only treating the symptoms, so the dis-ease is likely to manifest again, as I know from experience.

To truly get underneath a symptom, to get at the root, we need to consider every factor that might be contributing to the problem, as holistic practitioners understand. Gardeners also have an innate understanding of this. If your rose has black spot, it's no good just treating it with pesticides. It's also important to consider whether the plant is comfortable in its environment: does it have adequate nutrients, enough light, space and water? Is it infested with parasites? Is it happy where it is? I believe plants, trees and animals have a consciousness of their own. If they develop a problem, it will manifest physically to get attention. Just like our bodies.

It's my experience that our bodies are constantly sending us feedback. Often our lives are too crowded to listen to the quiet voice within, the one that tells us if we're off-balance. We live 'filled-full' kinds of lives in this twenty-first century Western world, but true 'fulfilment' can evade us. If we keep refusing to listen to minor symptoms, our bodies' dis-eases will become increasingly amplified in their seriousness until we *do* pay attention. We are all blessed with inner wisdom. It just takes the willingness to ask, listen, and sometimes wait for the answer.

We generally spend far more time worrying about what we put into our mouths, than we do about the words that come out of them. Of course, the food we eat, water we drink, social conditions, cellular inheritance and environment all have their part to play in our circumstances, but it's my firm conviction that we can more positively influence our quality of life when we consciously engage with our thoughts, feelings, beliefs and the expression of our truths.

Current scientific thought, pioneered by inspirational beings like Dr Candace Pert and Dr David Hamilton tells us that the body and mind are so intrinsically linked that science doesn't even bother to separate the two words anymore. So the 'bodymind' is the part of us that processes our thoughts and turns them into reality.

But where does that leave spirituality, inspiration, those enlightening experiences where we know beyond doubt who we are and why we're here? I would go one step further and encourage you to remember that we are three-part, or mindbodyspirit beings, and that we need to be resolving dis-ease on all these levels simultaneously. By dis-ease I'm not just referring to physical ailments. 'Ease' is our natural spiritual state, as anyone who has ever transcended their mortal form will know. It's difficult being attached to a body! They age, they leak, they need regular maintenance and many of us have additional physical challenges to work with in this lifetime.

It's no good just treating the physical form, although that might bring some temporary symptomatic relief. It's pointless just working with the mind, though many of us believe that this is the 'control centre' of the body because it's easy to get stuck there. And we can't expect to live a purely spiritual existence without nourishing the body and mind as well.

Creative intuition

For us to be truly well we need to feel whole. Only when the three aspects of us – mind, body and spirit – are in harmony do we experience that sense of 'rightness' that signifies we are 'on track', in concert with the universe.

More and more people are waking up to the fact that we are being limited to a miniscule percentage of our true potential. Not by governments or companies, terrorists or environmental threats. Not by our parents, our partners, our children, our religions or our jobs. Not even by our state of health. But by ourselves, by our inner conversations – those insidious internal saboteurs that make us question our own innate wisdom.

We're all familiar with that knowledgeable internal voice that nudges us to take an umbrella even though the sky is a cloudless blue, the surety we sometimes experience when we know who's calling before we pick up the phone, the 'gut' feeling that precedes decisions. It's the same inner guidance system, which keeps our hearts beating, regulates breathing, grows a baby and charts menstrual cycles with the moon.

We can also tap into our intuition to heal our bodies, come up with creative solutions to problems and infuse our lives with a sense of joy and purpose. It just takes a willingness to tune into this inner intelligence and the commitment to follow its guidance. Pretty soon we realize that we're creating our own map in life.

I once had a dream in which I was travelling on a fast-moving train. A small man came up to me and said, conspiratorially 'Want me to show you how to drive this thing?'

Well I was curious so I followed him through the carriage to a control panel, which I'd never noticed before. He showed me a computer screen with what looked like a floating glass ball in a dome alongside it.

I watched him hover his hand above the dome then pull back and slowly move his hand toward the ball again. As he did so a map appeared on the screen and zoomed in until I could see the track ahead and the trees whizzing by. Smiling, he invited me to try. I wanted to know why I would bother to drive the train, as someone else was obviously doing a good enough job. We were moving, the track was underneath us and I expected to arrive at my destination on time.

'Because it's your train,' he explained with some patience. 'You can get it to take you wherever you want.'

'Oh! But what about the tracks?' I asked.

'You lay the tracks as you go!' he laughed.

I awoke from that dream and then slipped straight into another with a similar theme. This time I was on an ocean liner, hanging up washing in the engine room. A cleaning lady came to me and handed me a key from the pocket of her apron.

'What's this?' I asked.

'That's the key to your ship.'

I was starting to catch on. 'Are you going to show me the controls?'

'Oh there aren't any controls as such, just this thing here.' And she used the key to open a cupboard housing what looked like a porthole.

'A window?'

'More of a GPS. You just look through here, decide where you want to go and your ship will take you there. She listens to your thoughts', she said smiling.

Now if that wasn't my inner wisdom sending me a clear message about tuning in and following my intuition, I don't know what is! Life is full of so many miracles and if we can only learn to trust ourselves and craft our stories with care, we'll be taken to magical places we only half dare to believe exist.

The process of life

This book will help you explore your inner terrain and take charge of the incessant internal dialogue that seems to scroll like ticker tape in your mind. If you take the time to engage with the processes sprinkled throughout the book, and commit to working on the words you use and the beliefs you hold, your actions will take care of themselves and your world will start to miraculously shape itself around your highest thoughts.

The result will be a deeper sense of peace and an unfolding feeling of awe at being a part of the process of life. As soon as you take responsibility for the role you are playing in your own mini-drama or full-length feature film, your health is bound to improve. When you start to turn old ideas on their heads and develop a new belief system that fully supports you, you may notice that the state of your bank account is dependent on how you're feeling about money and the degree of prosperity you feel you deserve – not the other way round. And when the words you speak have been considered and bathed in love before they're allowed to leave your lips (or fingertips), imagine how your relationships will improve.

So much of what we've learned has been passed on to us via words and stories, which hinge on others' beliefs, and many of us have never thought to question whether those ways of thinking still serve or limit us as full-grown adults. Occasionally we'll clear out our wardrobes, cull our emails and generally set our houses in order but how often do we give our beliefs a good airing?

This book takes a look at how we can use words to help or hinder, to expand or restrict our experience here on Earth.

As you move through some of the exercises, sometimes you may find yourself at the edge of your comfort zone. You might suddenly become distracted, very sleepy, upset or annoyed; start yawning a lot or develop an irritation within your body. That's a good sign. Please don't walk away at this point, as usually it's a signal that you're getting close to something that may have been causing you trouble in the past, perhaps without you even having been aware of it. Remember that no person, thought or situation has any power over you unless you decide that it has. Just remain as present as you can, breathe and commit to taking one step at a time. Just one step, that's all that's required. You'll know when you're ready to take the next one.

Above all, working on yourself and becoming conscious of the effect you are having on the world can be a fun process, a journey of discovery and wonder! Self-improvement can easily turn into addictive navel-gazing and become 'heavy' if we dwell too much on our emotional baggage. The aim is to intervene in our negative thought processes and *change* our way of communicating with ourselves and the world, not become bogged down in why we think or speak the way we do. Change your words to change your world. And remember to ask yourself at intervals: 'Will my words *improve* the silence?'

1
OUR STORY

....

'The biggest adventure you can take is
to live the life of your dreams.'

Oprah Winfrey

....

It was September 2002 and sunshine played through the trees at the back of the house. I pulled on my rucksack, opened the door and drank deeply in the vanilla-scented morning, taking in the hint of a nutty earth smell, a gentle reminder that the seasons were starting to turn.

Something felt different today. The leaves were etched against an impossibly blue sky, which somehow seemed closer. Everything had a message for me – I could feel my veins thrumming to an ancient beat – but much as I strained to hear, the only sound for miles was birdsong.

A curious squirrel stopped halfway along the five-bar gate into the garden and fixed me with an unflinching stare. 'Well, what're you waiting for?' he seemed to say before scurrying off.

I sighed and pushed through the tall grass into the woods beyond. As I got closer to the dry-stone wall bordering the back fields and bent down to scoop up some dry twigs, it occurred to me that Seth – my new boyfriend (and friend for the past 20 years) – was missing out. OK, we might be destitute and soon-to-be-homeless, but surely this beautiful morning was worth noticing?

I looked back at the low white Ayrshire cottage with its fading hanging baskets, and felt a warm swell of appreciation for everyone inside it: Seth, curled up in bed; his two beautiful daughters who stayed with us every weekend; his quiet sister Becky and her young son Josh. All of us squashed up into a single room so that we could make a hasty retreat from the creditors encircling us if necessary.

We had all once believed in our dream, swept along by a tide of enthusiasm. Some stalwart friends and colleagues still do, and we'll always be grateful to them. Two years previously I had moved to Scotland from England, totally burned out yet determined to follow my heart. Seth and I had moved in together and started a multimedia business with the shared ideal of making a difference in the world. Just at the time when Scotland had been labelled the 'sick man of Europe' we'd created some interactive software for kids, educating them in a fun way about nutrition and exercise, which was quickly adopted by Glasgow City Council and a handful of local celebrities.

Thinking our future was secure, we'd naively calculated a return of investment within two years, and borrowed to the hilt. It was to be another four years before the project was finally rolled out as part of the National Curriculum, by which time we'd lost our home, our energy, our solvency and most of our pride. But that's another story.

Standing in the hush of the woods that late September morning, arms and rucksack full of firewood, knowing it was time to move on, but not knowing where or how, I'd never felt so alive.

We'd been staying in the cottage for two months. Most days were the same. Get up, cold shower, a layering of whatever clothes you could find, a hasty mug of tea and piece of toast before it was time to face the creditor of the day. Seth would valiantly travel to Glasgow in the grim hope that a cheque or some good news would arrive (they never did) and that the bills wouldn't (they always did) while I would head to the woods to gather firewood for the open fire, the main source of heating in the cottage.

But this morning everything had changed. The night before, Becky had gently asked us to leave. The strain of living in a cramped house with two frantic adults and three lively kids was starting to show. This news had been too much for Seth who'd retreated to bed, determined to stay there for as long as possible. I'd left him under the covers that morning while I headed out, blithely convinced that something positive would come out of all this.

Tree of knowledge

A few weeks earlier when I'd been gathering firewood in the same spot, I had been drawn to a mammoth tree that seemed to explode out of the ground. She was a giant beech, dwarfing every tree for miles, shrouded in green mystery, and we've since renamed her 'Mama Beech'.

Having led the no-nonsense life of a senior executive in the newspaper industry and been the head of my own company up to this point, talking to trees had never really been part of my routine. So I'd put it down to sheer exhaustion when she started to speak inside my head!

'Sit down here, take a piece of paper, apply for your ideal life... and make sure you get it.' Her words, not mine. Stunned, and secretly feeling that I'd sunk to a new low, I had pulled a notebook from my pocket, sat down with my back against her trunk and started to write. 'Present tense,' she'd nudged.

About an hour later I'd filled several pages with stuff I hadn't even known I'd wanted. A large house that my friends and family could call home, set in a natural environment, surrounded by trees and fields. A healing room and somewhere I could write. I wanted a career that would combine the two (healing and writing), working from home and bringing in enough to live on. To have a dog... and marriage to Seth. Wow! What a fantasy!

So here I was, weeks later, standing in front of the same tree. 'Huh' I thought. 'So much for all that.' But as I turned to leave, I felt the word 'trust' directed at my back.

I dumped the wood at the front door, tapped on the bedroom window and called out that I was going for a walk. Silence. The car was still in the driveway.

Becky's old gatehouse cottage was rented from the laird of a rundown estate. Once known as 'the challenge', it's built on the crossing of two leylines, one of which runs through the ruins of Scotland's first Masonic lodge. The build-up of energy within the house is so powerful that you regularly have to knock a tapstone to release it, so it's a legendary healing and transformative place. It stands at the entrance to a square mile of indigenous and imported trees, undulating fields and a chuckling river that meanders through the grounds. The crowning glory of the estate is a mansion house, built around a twelfth-century keep, all of which had fallen into disrepair.

I chose the path toward the mansion house and was so absorbed in my thoughts that I didn't even hear the car pull up beside me. Peering out from the open window was Lina, the laird's wife. They'd assumed their inheritance a few months earlier and were about to renovate the house. Lina and I had shared stories over a few glasses of wine, and were just starting what would become a valued friendship.

'Hello darling! You look like you could do with a chat and a coffee! Jump in!' she trilled. We headed past the cracked, moss-covered tennis courts to her newly converted carriage house. Over a frothy coffee by the Aga in her big warm kitchen, Lina heard me out. I hadn't intended to be quite so thorough, but an hour had passed, the coffee was cold and I was still rattling on.

She looked at me thoughtfully, head to one side. 'Hmm. I've got some errands to run. Why don't you come with me? We'll talk as we go.' Her tone brooked no argument so I followed her out the door to the car. We pulled up outside the main house and she produced a huge bunch of keys. For the next half an hour I trailed her up four flights of stairs to the top of the house, through every room and back down to the bottom, talking all the way. We got to the kitchen before I drew breath. 'So... how would you like to live here darling?' she smiled.

'Here?' I repeated, uncomprehending.

'Yes here. In the East Wing?'

It was only then that I noticed the place was empty; I'd been so wrapped up in my story! I felt like someone had shaken fairy dust all over me and I didn't want the spell to break.

'I'd love to, but we could never afford it.'

'Look. I know the dreams you carry in your heart and I believe they'll happen. You've written them down haven't you? Why don't you go back to Seth, decide what you could afford and we'll put it to the Trust?'

I shivered. Trust ... there was that word again! I could hardly contain myself and after nearly knocking her over with my kiss, I thanked her and ran out the door, not stopping till I reached Becky's cottage.

Seth was still huddled under the covers and must've woken with a real shock when a blonde blur of breathless incoherence landed on him. When he'd extracted the story from the tumble of words that fell out of me, a slow smile spread across his face and we started to work out what we could afford.

But even with every penny we had left and the meagre income we were pulling in from scraps of work we'd managed to salvage, it was nowhere close to what we thought the Trust would accept.

The only solution was to call a mutual friend who was looking for a place to live. 'Pamela? What are you doing for lunch? Today. I only need 15 minutes! I promise you, you won't regret it!'

New beginnings

Pamela came out to see the house that evening, we pooled our resources, came up with a proposal and put it to the Trust that same week. Then, true to all manifestation techniques, we let go of the dream, as we were due to spend a week together in Germany working for Salem International, a children's charity that would become very important to us.

We asked everyone we knew to pray for us, or at least imagine us living there, which is really the same thing. One of our friends in Germany gave us hope, saying 'It's done. I can already see you living in the house.'

When we came home, a thick envelope was waiting for us – a six-month lease! I think we cried. We all moved in together the following week, November 2002 and, despite the fact that we only expected to be there for six months, we decided to unpack. Just as well really – we ended up living there for the next nine years.

The East Wing was a sprawling delight of idiosyncrasies. Added by the de Blair family in the 1700s, it was originally the nursery wing, and a joyful childlike energy still permeated some of the rooms. Because it had been a family home for the past 20 years, some of the larger pieces of furniture had just been left behind, probably because they were far too heavy to lift. One of my favourites was a huge oak chest with an ornate Harry Potter style key and the date 1795 among the intricate carvings that covered it.

As you entered the house by the heavy front door you were faced with a church pew, or settle as it's called in Scotland. There were coat pegs and shoe racks for about 20 pairs of shoes; perfect for all the friends we wanted to look after. The 70ft wood-panelled hallway peeked into the original stone-built keep, looking into a world gone by.

An antiquated industrial boiler tried its level best to heat the house in winter for the first few years of our tenancy, a pointless exercise considering the sash windows were single-glazed and leaked air like punctured lungs. The living room carpet was threadbare, the huge kitchen housed a lethal dumb waiter, which arced blue light if you so much as looked at it, the water ran alternately brown and orange, we were often without electricity and a working phone, plus we had a ghost cat, a leaky roof and a resident family of very cheeky mice.

We loved it.

We soon learned the true value of thick woollen sweaters, candles and hot water bottles. We knew the location of every charity shop and auction room within a five-mile radius, and how to make hearty soup from just about anything we could find. The mice had a lucky escape on more than one occasion! As they lived in the larder, which had a vent and a north-facing wall, I'm surprised they didn't freeze to death.

As you mounted the stairs to the first floor, two very stern-looking portraits of Colonel Blair and his wife, who lived in 'the Wing' during the early 1900s, critically appraised you. We never had the heart to take the pictures down, and fancifully imagined that the Colonel's eyes softened over the years, as he came to recognize the love and respect we held for his house. Either that or the glass needed dusting!

The double-aspect living room at the heart of the house overlooked the sweeping red gravel driveway and a clutch of 200-year-old towering redwoods. We spent many a cozy evening huddled around the open fire, playing cards, drinking wine and singing along to

Seth's guitar. For the first few years we couldn't afford a TV in that room, so homegrown entertainment became a necessity. A 4ft-square thick pine coffee table, the only piece of furniture Seth and I owned when we moved in, took pride of place in the centre of the room, surrounded by three deep comfy sofas, which crept closer to the fire as the nights drew in.

One of the 'understandings' of the estate was that we could help ourselves to any fallen wood, so we always had a full log basket. We learned to set 'single match' fires from the very best – Betty, the estate's 85-year-old housekeeper, whose secret recipe included corks and candle stubs.

Across the hall was the study, stuffed with book-laden shelves, computers and a tangle of cables, and graced with a small chandelier. Since we all intended to work from home when we moved in and there weren't enough desks, I commandeered a full-length mahogany claw-foot dining table and covered it with green baize. Here I would sit, tapping away at my computer, surrounded by inspirational photos and affirmations, dramatically lit by an Anglepoise lamp. Friends used to joke that I could run the world from my huge desk, and I came home one day to find an enormous laminated map of the world covering the wall behind it. All I needed to complete the picture was a fluffy white cat and a leather chair!

Next door was the first of four bedrooms, a peaceful pale yellow room with a mahogany fireplace and writing bureau, overlooking the river. At the back of the house on the first floor there was a bathroom and a tiny pantry kitchen, complete with original Butler sink.

Pamela soon got used to her enormous en-suite bedroom, which, with its two large wardrobes, kingsize bed, fireplace and chest of drawers, was bigger than entire flats she'd been viewing. Seth and I settled into one of the top floor attic rooms with a sloping ceiling, which I loved because it overlooked the outdoor pool and gardens, and the kids shared its twin facing the river and tree-lined bank.

But the room that really took your breath away was the Cecily Blair room on the second floor. Crowned by a magnificent carved four-poster bed, elegant chaise longue and intricately crafted fireplace, this was the epitome of bridal suites. When the main house was renovated this room was reclaimed as the master bedroom, but for two blissful years we could gaze on it and pretend it was ours. I would often envisage celebrating my first book signing with a Champagne reception there.

An ideal life

In those early days, even though we had absolutely no money and very few prospects, we felt like millionaires. Whatever we needed seemed to manifest itself almost instantly. Washing machines, sofas, fridges, TVs, computers, even cars would turn up. If something went wrong, there was always someone around to help fix it. Everyone was willing to share. And if we were feeling low, all we had to do was walk outside and look around. In return we fed anyone who came through the door, listened to their troubles, gave healing treatments and helped where we could.

It was important to me that we lived according to the vision I'd had under Mama Beech. The house seemed to come alive when people visited and the East Wing was rapidly becoming a place where people felt they could relax and be restored. My mantra has always been 'you are safe and you are loved', a phrase I try to build into all my Reiki treatments. In time, the very walls seemed to emanate this message. When people came to stay, they didn't want to leave in a hurry. It had become a healing centre by word of mouth alone.

I firmly believe that thoughts and feelings create your reality. I also believe that if you write down your dreams or out-picture them, it brings you one step closer to achieving them. The very act of believing something long enough to write it down if you're a wordy person, or create a storyboard if you're more visual, or even record your own voice telling a story in the present tense if that inspires you, seems to shift the energy toward creation.

Then we have to let our vision go, which is often thought of as the hardest part. The mistake we tend to make is taking it all too seriously. I like to treat this part as a game, pretending I've entered a universal competition, which I can't possibly lose. Whatever comes back will be OK. After all, I also believe that we are always in the right place at the right time, with the people and circumstances necessary for our growth. We just need to learn to trust the process. Even if this is not true, *what if* you believed it was? Your life would definitely change for the better.

So one year later, we were settled in Blair, with no idea of how we were going to earn enough money to pay the rent and feed ourselves. We looked out on paradise each day but were bankrupt. It had taken all our inner resources to get through the past year, with the disappointments of business to contend with and, to be honest, we needed time to regroup and re-energize.

While Seth valiantly went off to work each day to keep the software project alive, Pamela and I would shut ourselves away in the study, wearing fingerless gloves and big jumpers and tap away at our keyboards. A dear friend Kenny sold his flat and moved in to help with the finances, and keep us entertained with his pithy Scottish humour.

We'd decided to take in any work that came our way. By day we got stuck into audio-typing, funding proposals, magazine articles, even organizing business lunches. By night we would don our black and white uniforms and head next door to the mansion house where we would greet and serve the well-heeled guests who were starting to stay at Blair.

Isn't it strange how we bring into being what we have inside us? Although I had been a high-flying executive managing teams of people who were older and more experienced than me, the perception I was carrying around that our business had 'failed' was colouring my judgment. I had become self-critical, convinced I would never be able to cope with work that demanded any more of me than washing dishes. Even though the house we lived in was living proof that affirmations and positive thinking worked, if I look back to the thoughts I was carrying around in my head at that time, I'm surprised by their negativity.

Where attention goes, energy flows

Thoughts such as *'There's never enough money'*, *'I'll never get a good job'*, *'Nobody's interested in what I have to say/write about'*, *'This good fortune won't last'*, and other variations on the theme of *'I'm not good enough'*, stopped me from attracting meaningful, well-paid work for a long time. But one daily practice I did maintain was saying 'thank you'. Every time I walked outside and breathed the fresh clean air, or leaned against an ancient tree, I said thank you. And really, that's all a prayer or affirmation is. It's acknowledging that something in your experience is good and that you're grateful for it. It's true; where attention goes, energy flows.

One thing that truly warmed my heart was seeing the pleasure that others derived from the house and its surroundings. Friends would come for the weekend and not want to leave. In fact some of them never left! No matter how stressed they were when they arrived, they would always go away with a new perspective, a sense of being restored.

We were living simply, growing organic vegetables, cooking up big soups, stews and 'heaters', as they're known in Scotland: gathering firewood and making our own entertainment. We recycled and composted as much as we could, shared what we had and laughed a lot. If we could help anyone out we did, and we stopped being afraid of receiving aid in return – a hard lesson for any independent person to learn.

We owned nothing – even the car was repossessed eventually – but still felt rich beyond measure. I remember sitting with Seth on the riverbank one glorious summer's day (yes, we do get them in Scotland) and asking where he would live if he won the lottery. As we gazed at the back of the house, the answer was obvious. We were already living the life of our dreams. OK so we didn't own it, but really that just meant we didn't have the cost and responsibility of maintaining it. The only regret we had was that by not having any extra money, we were unable to help others as much as we wanted.

We had no idea what the future held: that within ten years our collective dreaming would help us serve the world in ways we hadn't imagined. That we would be able to set up our own branch of an international charity alongside some of our closest friends and help spread a message of peace and hope from our little corner of this beautiful planet. With the benefit of hindsight, all I can say is 'your words and visions are creative. Be careful what you wish for ...'

2

HEALTH

....

'A healthy outside starts from
the inside.'

Robert Urich

....

One of my strongest beliefs is that what you give out comes back to you multiplied. This is just as true of thoughts and feelings as of actions. While I was bombarding the universe with thoughts of 'I am not good enough,' 'I don't deserve it', 'There's never enough,' and so on, that is what was coming right back at me.

This universal intelligence, of which we are all a part, is so faithful it reflects back exactly what you tell it. If you say 'I want' it will respond 'so you do.' And there you are, stuck in a state of wanting. If, however, you affirm that you already have whatever it is you think you need, the chances are you'll either be prompted to recognize that you really do already have it (usually by being stretched in some way) or you will attract it to you.

The trick is to appreciate whatever it is you already 'have', be it harmonious relationships (even if it's only with your dog at this stage), sound health, financial abundance, a great job, etc.

While I was affirming for the ideal house back in September 2002, I was also blessing all the houses I'd lived in before, as well as feeling grateful for the opportunity we'd been given to stay with Becky for longer than expected. It's the feeling that's important, and gratitude seems to be the universe's most fertile soil.

If you take the time to really examine whatever it is you have in your life, you'll probably realize that on some level you expect to have it. If it's something that's been with you for a while, it's usually because you're comfortable with it, or it's helping you understand something.

For example, for years I had struggled with various health problems. As a 'driven' executive, I suffered from irritable bowel syndrome and, eventually, complete exhaustion, or burnout. When I first moved to my new life in Scotland, all these symptoms miraculously disappeared and I felt healthier than I had for years. My life was working on all levels.

After our business crashed, my self-esteem plummeted, my relationship with myself and others suffered and, of course, I created a series of 'joyless' conditions in my body. First it was *Candida albicans*, a yeast overgrowth, which makes many women's, lives miserable. Then it was a thyroid imbalance, which changed the texture of my skin, made my hair fall out, increased my weight, drained all my energy and stopped me thinking clearly. I was convinced there was something seriously wrong because it changed so many systems I had previously taken for granted within my body.

After that I grew a uterine fibroid so large that people thought I was pregnant and started offering me seats on trains! An ultrasound scan showed the tumour was the equivalent of an 18-week foetus. I was very self-conscious of my protruding belly and, what was worse, the incredibly heavy periods accompanying the fibroid made me severely anaemic, which in turn increased the bleeding. At the lowest point of this condition my doctor cautioned me not to climb stairs or do any housework because I was running an acute risk of a heart attack. I was 35 years old.

In all these cases, it was only when I took the trouble to really go within and get to the root of the problem, the 'heart of the matter' that my body would heal. Dr Deepak Chopra coined the wonderful phrase 'every cell in your body is eavesdropping on your internal conversation'. Although diet and lifestyle changes certainly help, I am convinced that clearing and releasing thought patterns and emotions, which no longer serve us, is an intrinsic part of the process if we are to heal on all three levels.

The body is a living pharmacy

Whatever your body creates, it can heal. It is my belief that spirit holds the original blueprint of perfect health for each of our bodies. Dr Candace Pert's groundbreaking studies of neuropeptides and her research into opiate receptors reveal that there is a corresponding receptor for every drug known to man on the surface of each cell. So we can generate feel-good chemicals and, if we know how to tap into this healing storehouse, we can heal without the drugs. It's just a question of knowing how ...

Plant medicine, thankfully, is coming back into our culture. There are herbs for every condition and the knowledge of how to use them was passed down from woman to woman through generations until recently. Where pharmaceutical drugs are designed to scientifically emulate the physical properties of plants and can be very effective if used carefully, the holistic, energetic quality of the whole plant is lost, creating inconvenient and sometimes dangerous side effects.

I am not unrealistic. I believe that most healing practices have their advantages. If someone broke their leg I wouldn't hang about giving them Reiki, I'd get them to the local hospital as soon as I could. (Though it might be a good idea to travel with them and give them Reiki on the way to keep them calm.) Herbs, diet, relaxation techniques, exercise, surgery and even drugs can all be effective in treating health disorders.

But the key factor for me, which is so often overlooked, is going within to receive the message. Louise Hay spent many years compiling her 'little blue book', a catalogue of symptoms and the probable emotional contributing factors underlying them. When she condensed them down, she found that most imbalances in the body could be attributed to just three primary emotions – guilt, anger and fear. I have found this to be true in the majority of cases when treating patients in my healing practice too.

If anger is held onto and stored in the body it will eventually 'erupt' as a burning or itching feeling – the medical term is usually a condition ending in '-itis'. Boils, cysts, rashes and fevers are all symptoms of anger and it can show up emotionally as impatience, irritation, frustration, resentment, bitterness, jealousy or criticism. Fear often manifests as tension, anxiety, worry, doubt or feelings of unworthiness. Guilt and resentment literally 'eat away' at your body if they becomes habitual, and can manifest as cancer. Women, and mothers in particular, are experts at carrying around suitcases of self-blame and guilt, often unconsciously.

It's time to let go of all blame and guilt.

Inner healing

Healing is all about creating the conditions necessary for the body to heal itself. Our inner wisdom will do the rest. High temperatures are the body's way of purifying itself.

Vomiting and diarrhoea are the same. Pain is usually a symptom of guilt and where the pain occurs can tell us a great deal about the source of the problem. For example, headaches are about our egos punishing us. Pain in the neck can be issues with flexibility, discomfort in the stomach difficulty 'processing' new ideas, and lower back pain is usually about feeling unsupported or having money or relationship worries.

I once walked to work behind a rather large lady with very swollen ankles and wrists, who was having some difficulty walking. Having just returned from a week's training in Louise Hay's philosophy, I was curious as to why the lady should be storing so much fluid. Then I noticed she was wearing a conference badge stating 'Complaints Management Committee'. Louise's little blue book suggests that 'holding onto criticism' causes swelling. No wonder the lady was so uncomfortable! I was very tempted to stop her in the street and advise her to 'get pissed off' and let all the complaints leave her body, but was deterred by the fact that she might think I was crazy.

Listen to your body

The heart has long been touted as being the barometer of our emotions. We talk about our hearts being full, broken, open, closed, heavy, light and so on. We even refer to a heart 'attack', suggesting it has turned on us. In truth, it's more likely to have given up trying to pump life energy around our bodies after we have squeezed all the joy out of our lives.

All these symptoms are trying to get our attention, telling us to slow down, change our pace, go inside and reflect. Yet we think we're superhuman. Rather than stop or give into our bodies' demands, we pop a pill, rev up on caffeine and carry on with even more determination.

In the macho culture that has become the working norm in Europe and America, we work longer and longer hours, hoping for more recognition, satisfaction, reward and productivity. Childbearing age is increasing in the developed world as more and more women put off raising a family in favour of pursuing their careers. The family unit is stretched to breaking point as men and women spend more time working so they can pay for more consumer goods, and teachers are dissolving under the pressure of having to be substitute parents, psychologists, counsellors and, more often than not, policemen.

Resting is seen as weak in our culture as we strive to stuff more and more into the same number of hours we've always had. But I've got news – days aren't getting any longer! The more pressure we put on ourselves, particularly if we're feeling trapped in any way or are out of alignment with our deeper values and purpose, the more likely it is that our health will suffer.

We can't ignore our state of health for too long. When we do crash, it's likely to be spectacular, as that's the only way our bodies can get our attention. Illness has become a socially acceptable way of saying 'no' without causing offence. Many of us lack assertiveness to such an extent that we hide behind our ailments. How often have you pulled a 'sickie' at work or got yourself out of doing something because you didn't feel well?

A lot of the illnesses we think of as physical are often actually an emotional or even spiritual malaise. Our society is geared towards external realities and therefore external solutions, so it's only natural for us to want to be 'fixed' by someone or something outside of ourselves. We'll visit a doctor, research alternative therapies on the internet, read a book written by an expert. But no one can really interpret another's disease. Healing is a personal journey and meaning can take time to unfold. Ultimately we all face death, and it will be the spirit that decides at which points we heal or self-destruct, but we do have a lot of innate power which can determine the quality of our lives while we're here.

UK amateur athlete Jane Tomlinson was diagnosed with incurable metastatic breast cancer in 2000, and told she had just six months to live. Despite this bleak prognosis, she dedicated the rest of her life to raising money for charity and over the next seven years successfully completed the London Marathon, the Great North Run and the Ironman UK Triathlon, as well as cycling 4,200 miles across the US on a nine-week fundraiser. In that time she raised over £1,500,000 for charity and inspired millions of people along the way. Although she died of her disease in 2007, no one could claim her story to be one of failure. Motivated by a desire to leave her beloved family with some fantastic memories, Jane outlived her prognosis and left behind an inspirational legacy. We can all make a unique difference.

The power to harm or heal

A word about the medical profession: I fully support doctors, nurses, surgeons and other health professionals and know that the vast majority have been drawn to their profession by a desire to help, to heal. However, what frustrates me is the absolute mantle of authority we have placed on them. In Western society, medics have overtaken even priests in our esteem! If a doctor prescribes a drug and we believe it will heal us, the likelihood is it will. The same can be said of a placebo, a sugar-coated pill with no active ingredients, revealing that it is our beliefs that hold the potency.

Medical professionals have a duty of care. We used to speak of a doctor's 'bedside manner' and the modern Hippocratic oath states:

> '... I will remember that there is art to medicine as well as science, and that warmth, sympathy, and understanding may outweigh the surgeon's knife or the chemist's drug.'

A study by the University of York featured in *The Lancet* in 2001 showed that enhancing patient expectations through positive information about the treatment of the illness while providing support or reassurance significantly influenced health outcomes. Conversely, if our physician tells us we have terminal cancer and only have two months to live, a lot of us will give up. Talk about giving away our power!

Jane is a registered nurse and health visitor. Having longed for a child of her own, she was delighted when her daughter Maria was born, but joy turned to heartbreak when Maria was diagnosed with cancer aged 11 months. Having also trained as a clinical hypnotherapist, Jane was acutely aware of the effect words have on the unconscious mind, and was determined to protect her daughter from any negativity surrounding her condition. She opted for a conventional course of treatment including chemotherapy, but insisted that every health professional and adult that came into contact with her daughter would only talk about the cancer and her prognosis in positive terms, even while Maria was under anaesthetic.

Jane also wove hypnosis techniques into Maria's bedtime stories, and taught her empowering self-hypnosis techniques for pain relief and visualization. Fifteen years later, Maria is still in remission.

While Jane was training to be a hypnotherapist, another remarkable thing occurred. A previous car accident had left her right arm incapacitated, to the extent that she had no sensation from midway up her arm to the tips of her fingers. She was always burning herself in the kitchen. At the time, her doctor had categorically told her that her arm would not recover as the nerves and tissues were too damaged to repair themselves. However, during her hypnotherapy training, one of the exercises involved inducing trance and numbing her left arm using the power of suggestion. At the end of the exercise, Jane's tutor asked the group to use the phrase 'I now remove all previous hypnotic suggestions from your arm.' As luck would have it, the partner she was working with mistakenly removed all hypnotic suggestions from *both* arms. Immediately Jane started to feel a tingling in her right arm and burst into tears of joy. Miraculously, over the course of the next few weeks she regained full sensation in her 'irreparable' arm!

Jane's story is a powerful reminder of how much store we put in doctors' words and the effect they have on our unconscious minds when we are at our most receptive and vulnerable. Our life can literally hang in the balance depending on our response to their prognosis. In this litigious age it does make you wonder how many health professionals are so fearful of being sued that they give the worst-case scenario to protect themselves.

Re-balancing

Around the time I developed *Candida albicans* I was feeling really low. There was a huge lack of trust in my relationship with Seth and others, some of it justified, some of it my perception. Losing a business, particularly one you've run with your partner, is bound to bring up issues of blame, feelings of failure and a decline in confidence.

Dietary changes certainly helped. I switched to a virtually sugar-free diet full of raw foods and garlic. It was January so luckily there weren't many parties in the diary! I invested in the highest quality organic multi-vitamin within my budget and took daily probiotics. I drank only water and herbal tea and made sure I walked everywhere and went to bed early. After a month of this I lost a stone in weight ... and most of my friends!

I was utterly miserable, a real grump. When you deprive your body of sugar and caffeine, at first your serotonin levels drop. This is the real detox stage when your body chucks out all the old junk. Usually your skin suffers, you feel lethargic and if you've been taking caffeine on a daily basis you can experience horrible headaches. It's important to support your liver and colon at this stage, as they will be responsible for eliminating most of the toxins and need to be in the best of health. I would recommend a one-off colon, liver and kidney cleanse to kick-start the whole process. If colonics aren't your thing, raw fruit and vegetable juices can be just as effective.

Thankfully the detox 'hangover' doesn't last long. By the end of the month everything was starting to improve and my symptoms had reduced. After three months even carrots tasted like nectar and I was bursting with health and energy. And because my system was so much more robust and vital, it was possible to gradually introduce more foods back into my diet with no adverse side effects.

Although this was a powerful re-balancing of my physical body, I was also aware that remaining symptom-free would take more than just a nutritional overhaul. There was some serious emotional and mental house cleaning to be done. It was spring, a very symbolic time for clearing out the old and making room for the new so I set aside an hour a day to get in touch with my inner self.

Each evening, around the time the 'old' me would have been enjoying a glass of wine, I would take myself off to the bedroom, plump up the cushions on the bed and settle in for a meditation. Oh wow. The first sessions were like eavesdropping on a bitchy conversation. I couldn't believe how negative my self-talk had become! *'He never supports me, it's always down to me to make things right, this house is too big to keep clean, nobody cares ...'* and other such selfish drivel. I made a conscious decision to stop my negative thinking ... and then promptly forgot to do it!

Months later when I was diagnosed with an underactive thyroid and a uterine fibroid the size of a melon, the doctors I saw wanted to a) put me on thyroid drugs for the rest of my life, b) induce the menopause to shrink the fibroid or c) perform a hysterectomy. When

I told them I intended to heal my condition without recourse to any of those measures, they looked at me with a mixture of scorn and pity.

Again dietary changes helped, supplemented by some potent herbs, exercise and massage techniques. I also stopped drinking water from plastic bottles after uncovering some worrying research about xenoestrogens. But all along my inner wisdom was telling me the two were connected with frustrated creativity and emotions that I'd stuffed down inside myself for years.

As a Reiki practitioner I was aware that the second and fifth chakras were connected and imbalances in either could affect the other. The throat chakra is about self-expression and the sacral chakra about creativity. At the time both these conditions manifested, I was working in a 9 to 5 job in a multinational organization, which left me with little room for personal creativity and individuality. I was also carrying around a truckload of resentment. On a fundamental level, I knew that this sense of not being in alignment, together with my poor self-talk was adversely affecting my health.

Time to change

Here's a startling fact: fibroid tumours affect 30 per cent of women, many of whom are unaware they even have them. They are almost always benign, sometimes symptom-free and can lay undetected for years. They are also currently responsible for a third of all hysterectomies. A hysterectomy is a major operation with a considerable recovery time and a surgical complication rate of between 40 and 50 per cent. Many surgeons opt to remove the uterus and frequently the ovaries in preference to a myomectomy (surgical removal of the fibroid alone). This is despite the emerging research, which suggests that removal of the uterus, and ovaries might be detrimental to women's long-term health and can accelerate the aging process.

When you're faced with a monthly episode of feeling as though you're bleeding to death and are unable to walk for one day in every 28, it's actually a tempting prospect to let someone just 'whip it all out' and have done with it. Unless your condition is life threatening, however, and especially if you still want to have children, I would urge you to explore the other choices even if you do finally decide that major surgery is the best option for you.

Fibroids strike at the heart of a woman's femininity, her creative centre. As women we have a tendency to take a hurt from a person or a situation and nurse it until it takes up too much space in our wombs and lives.

Think of a pearl – it started out as a piece of grit that just got polished until it became precious! Same thing with slights and insults, but the difference is we nurture them until *we* become precious! I can't deny that I had become a walking example of this theory. If you re-read the thought processes I was carrying around then, you'll see the evidence was right there!

Dr Christiane Northrup, author of *Women's Bodies, Women's Wisdom* discusses fibroids in the light of unbirthed creativity. She talks about unfulfilling jobs and relationships, and issues around reproduction and motherhood. Louise Hay refers to fibroids as 'nursing a hurt from a partner' and speaks of heavy bleeding as being 'joy running out of the body'. Fibroids are extremely common in the Afro-Caribbean community where they are often labelled the 'he-done-me-wrong' syndrome.

Feeling overwhelmed or under pressure to 'fix' everything is a classic bond amongst fibroid sufferers and it's easy to see why such a fast-paced environment could be building more problems for future multi-tasking generations.

Some women with fibroids have internal conflicts about their sexuality, which they may have never explored and I know of others who have terminated a pregnancy without resolving the accompanying guilt. Many feel resentful that they have given up their own dreams for somebody else's and not been appreciated for it. Whatever the issue, it is usually connected with the expression of a woman's creativity.

The emotional 'profile' of someone with fibroids is likely to be an independent but sensitive woman, someone who is used to being self-reliant. There is a tendency to need to make things happen, to be 'ballsy' and 'gutsy' and some of the other qualities traditionally attributed to a man. When I was diagnosed with my fibroid, a friend who knows and loves me joked 'I wondered how long it would take you to try and make a baby on your own!' Hmm. Truth hurts.

Women's creativity is fundamentally different from a man's. Not to put too fine a point on it, when a man sows a creative seed it is very much in the moment whereas a woman's ideas and problem-solving abilities benefit from gestation. Of course we are all part feminine, part masculine but too often I have tried to succeed in a man's world by emulating men's behaviour. With the wisdom of hindsight it's clear to me how much more advantageous it would have been to have used my ovarian power and spent a bit more time creating a labour of love instead of constantly moving onto the next thing.

The thyroid, a butterfly-shaped gland at the base of the throat, is your body's regulator. It controls metabolism through the secretion of thyroid hormones and can be underactive (hypothyroidism) or overactive (hyperthyroidism). Not much is known for certain about what causes disturbances in the thyroid gland – autoimmune conditions, hereditary predisposition and dietary deficiency can all contribute.

In metaphysical terms, any imbalance around the throat area is concerned with self-expression, and thyroid problems, according to Louise Hay and others, symbolize feeling creatively stifled.

Orthodox medicine does recognize that imbalance in this gland can cause havoc with internal homeostatic systems, and accepts that prolonged stress can be a major factor.

Cortisol is a stress hormone, manufactured in the adrenal glands in response to stressors, which increases the efficiency of thyroid hormone. A physiologic amount – not too high and not too low – of cortisol is required for normal thyroid function. Too much of the stress hormone will create a condition of thyroid resistance whereby thyroid hormone levels remain normal but tissues fail to respond as effectively to the thyroid signal as they should. Perhaps more worryingly this resistance also applies to all other hormones, e.g. insulin, progesterone, oestrogens, testosterone and even cortisol itself.

When stress hits the adrenal glands, if they are fatigued from long-term abuse (classic burn-out), they can be unable to produce enough cortisol. Alternatively, chronic stress elevates cortisol levels to such an extent that you start getting resistance from hormone receptors throughout your body. In either case thyroid hormones become inefficient and thyroid activity is thrown off-balance.

Cortisol naturally fluctuates throughout the day, being lowest at 2 a.m. when the body is regenerating and highest in the morning when you need to get out of bed. Melatonin is the body's regenerator and works hard in the early hours to repair tissues and cells. If cortisol levels remain unnaturally high due to stress, melatonin production will be inhibited and not enough growth hormone or thyroid-stimulating hormone will be produced.

It goes without saying therefore that decreasing stress and following a 'sensible' lifestyle with enough regular sleep is vital to general, and especially hormonal, health.

Healing my condition certainly took patience and

understanding. By finally going within and truly listening to my body's messages I was able to take corrective action on the physical, mental/emotional and spiritual levels. My body healed from the thyroid imbalance over the course of a year, without recourse to any of the drugs or treatments proposed to me by my doctors. The fibroid took a lot longer and I eventually resorted to minor surgery in the form of uterine artery embolization to improve my quality of life while I worked on addressing the underlying emotional causes. Even though the operation was 100 per cent successful, it took a further two years for the fibroid to dissolve, much to the astonishment of my surgeon – even he urged me to 'let go of whatever you're hanging onto!' Once again it was only after I'd got to the heart of the matter and forgiven myself for an earlier termination that I was able to finally heal on all levels.

The human body is a far more sophisticated healing mechanism than we give it credit for. Every second, of every day, we are creating a new body. With every breath, we take in many billions of atoms, which will eventually make up our cells and tissues. As we exhale, we exchange atoms with everyone else, a neat little reminder that we truly are all one!

You create a new stomach lining every five days, a whole new skin every month, a liver every six weeks and a skeleton every three months. Within just one year, you will have replaced 98 per cent of all the atoms in your body!

So who says we can't reinvent ourselves? It's my experience that we can if we are willing to look within rather than outside ourselves for answers and change the way we talk to and about ourselves. The following chapters show you how ...

3

GETTING TO THE HEART OF THE MATTER

'Who looks outside, dreams; who
looks inside, awakes.'

Carl Jung

We are infinitely creative and powerful beings if we ally ourselves with the power that created us. We've become disconnected from this wisdom, the still small voice within, and have forgotten our inner compass. We need to get to the heart of the matter to discern what's right for us and remember we are spiritual beings having a human experience, not the other way round.

The mind thinks its job is to think up solutions to imagined problems; however its real job is to receive from the spirit and translate that into action. If we would only realize that every thought we have is creating our reality and every thought we've ever had has given us our life experiences so far, we'd be inspired to take the reins of this wonderful instrument called the mind and use our imagination to create the life of our dreams.

Take a minute to look around the room. Everything began as a thought in someone's mind. I recently had what I can only call an outer body experience, made all the more bizarre by the fact I was doing something very ordinary at the time. I'd just finished washing my hands after a visit to the bathroom and was reaching for a towel, when I realized I could see straight through it to the towel rail behind! Turning to look at the rest of the room I discovered everything was transparent – it was as if, for a few brief seconds, all the material objects surrounding me were just thought forms, blueprints. Oddly, rather than freaking me out, the experience gave me a tangible sense of relief! It made me realize that we really can create anything we can think if we believe in it. Everything we can imagine already exists in the spiritual realm. Our job is to express it in the physical world.

So how do we do that?

We do that by getting quiet, stilling the mind, and contacting the silence within. During a typical session at one of my clinics we take an inner journey together, a guided visualization that helps you get in touch with your own wisdom. I would like to share this with you.

Creative visualization

First, raise your vibration by putting your attention on the crown chakra – the point at the very top of your head – and feel your thoughts lift. This is the energetic point from which Eastern traditions would say we receive our highest wisdom. If you're clouded by negative thoughts here, substitute thoughts that make you feel good, for example, 'I am love'. Then ask internally to make contact with a higher power.

Next bring your attention to the heart chakra in the centre of the chest on your breastbone and feel it opening like a flower. Imagine yourself sitting in a throne at the centre of your heart and beam love toward that inner self. When you have accumulated enough love and your heart feels full, let the energy of love flow between your heart and crown chakras and send love to that higher power.

Disconnect yourself from having to be in control of the process or the outcomes. Leave that to the universe. It's not your job to work out the hows and whens! Now focus on whatever it is you want to bring into being. Use only positive imagery when making your request. Only plant the perfect seed within your heart and see it really clearly. So rather than ask to be healed of disease, see yourself manifesting perfect health. Instead of asking not to be poor, imagine abundance flowing freely into your life.

Give absolutely no thought or attention to the situations or habits you want to discard – you have outgrown them; just like old clothes you no longer need them. Visualize whatever it is you feel you're lacking as a shape or mould, which needs to be filled. Then imagine that need being filled with a magical substance, perhaps a shimmering golden light. Say to yourself: 'Let there be ...' followed by whatever the ideal is. Then say 'It's done and it is good', or simply 'Thank you'.

The trick here is to know absolutely that you have already received what you've asked for and then let go of the need for it. I know that possibly sounds like a big fat lie at the beginning and when your back's against the wall it can be difficult to imagine yourself in a positive situation. But the truth is that the more clearly you can see and feel yourself as being fully healthy, rich with prosperity, happy in love, etc., the quicker you'll be able to bring that into your reality. The universe can only give you what you expect to receive. If there are still blank spaces within you when you've imagined your ideal in as much detail as you can, fill them with thoughts that make you feel good.

I don't like to foster dependency on anything or anyone out-with this wisdom – you already have all the resources you need within. My clients generally need only two or three sessions to get the hang of this technique and I encourage them to practise at home. It might help at first to set aside 15 minutes each morning as soon as you wake up and again before you drop off to sleep at night. Sitting or lying down is fine, though if you practise every day soon you'll be able to do this while you're walking around going about your day.

Whatever you've asked for might show up immediately or it might take a while. It usually depends on how deserving you consider yourself to be. If it doesn't manifest straight away don't go asking again. Just give thanks and trust it will happen when the time is right. The universe will work out the details.

One note of caution: if your thoughts are destructive they *will* come back on you. Energy sent out has to return – usually with gathered strength. If your thoughts carry the intention of good for all, the energy that comes back will be beneficial.

Visualize your success

Many successful athletes, actors, businesspeople and health professionals have used creative visualization and mental rehearsal for many years. While actors and businesspeople might make use of the techniques to prepare for performances or presentations, athletes will use it to achieve peak performance in their sport, remembering previous wins to build a strong picture of success.

Jack Nicklaus, Tiger Woods and Michael Jordan are among the athletes that are known to have practised visualization techniques and the following saying is attributed to three-time World Heavyweight Boxing Champion, Muhammad Ali:

'Champions aren't made in gyms. Champions are made from something they have deep inside them – a desire, a dream, a vision.'

Tiger Woods was taught as a boy by his father how to visualize exactly where he wanted the golf ball to go and Arnold Schwarzenegger has used the power of his imagination to become Mr Universe five times and Mr Olympia six times, as well as holding down a career as a movie superstar, successful businessman and governor of California. When he was very young he used to visualize being and having everything he'd ever wanted and wouldn't give doubt a moment's thought. Most importantly he would imagine in advance how he would feel when he'd achieved his dreams.

If you don't believe you can visualize, please humour me for a second. Just close your eyes and imagine your front door. What colour is it? Where's the doorbell? If you can see something as everyday as this, you'll have no trouble visualizing your ideal life! And if you start practising, you'll be in good company – Alexander Graham Bell, Isaac Newton, Albert Einstein, Ludwig Van Beethoven and Martin Luther King Jr are also known to have visualized their successes.

Research shows that visualization can profoundly enhance physical practice and creativity because the brain does not clearly distinguish between real and vividly imagined experiences. The trick seems to be introducing all your senses – allow yourself to see, feel, taste, smell and touch the dream. It follows that if you spend your time thinking about rich, positive experiences your brain will develop its 'rich, positive experience' neural pathway and you'll begin to believe that they've already happened.

In the 1960s Professor L. V. Clark of Wayne State University conducted an interesting experiment[1]. He studied two groups of basketball players over a two-week period. One group practised shooting free throws every morning while the second group visualized making the shots without physically doing it. After two weeks, both groups had improved their free-throw shooting, proving just how powerful the imagination can be.

What's your desired outcome?

Whatever the desired outcome, the visualization process seems to be the same.

---

1 Extracted from *Nexus Magazine*, Volume 12, Number 3 (Apr–May 2005) by Paul Pearsall PhD, Gary E. Schwartz PhD, Linda G. Russek PhD

STEP 1: SET YOUR INTENTION AND WRITE IT DOWN

After you've decided which area of your life you want to focus on – work, play, health, relationships, family, money, etc., – write it down. Nothing too lengthy, bullet points will do. This is a crucial step in visualization and is often forgotten. Not only does it help focus your mind, but it can also act as a memory jogger if you drift off in your thoughts. Most importantly write down how you'd feel if you had achieved your dreams.

STEP 2: RELAX

Your body and mind are at their most receptive when they're fully relaxed, so when you're clear about your goal, push away the piece of paper and close your eyes. Concentrating on deep breathing or listening to binaural beats can help calm your senses and soothe your mind.

STEP 3: START VISUALIZING

Open your eyes and review your notes. Now you're ready to realize your dreams. Close your eyes and see yourself clearly in your vision. Where are you? Who else is there with you? Go right into the details and notice how you act differently in your dream. If any critical thoughts come in just thank them and turn them away. Don't worry too much if the dream seems far removed from your current reality – we're planting a seed, which will grow with practice.

STEP 4: BRING YOUR VISION TO LIFE

Now bring in all your senses. What are you hearing, seeing, feeling, tasting, touching? What does success smell like? Intensify the sensations of success until you feel as if you'd already achieved your dreams. This is the success image you can carry with you like a snapshot.

STEP 5: CREATE A REWARD VISION

Don't forget to reward yourself! Picture yourself celebrating with friends and family, smiling and laughing. Laugh out loud if you like. This will anchor the feeling and provide an extra incentive for getting there.

Five or ten minutes a day is enough to create this reality quite quickly once you've been through the process once or twice. See yourself overcoming obstacles and distractions easily. If it helps you can visualize your success movie running on a large screen in front of you. You'll soon discover what works best for you.

STEP 6: MAKE A GRATITUDE JOURNAL

A gratitude journal is another useful tool for manifesting

your dreams. Gratitude is the fertile soil of manifestation where you can plant the seeds of your dreams and watch them grow. Even if your life feels a bit like a blues melody and your health is suffering, you've just lost your job, your partner has walked out on you or any combination of life's other myriad problems, I urge you to focus on something you're grateful for right now.

Get yourself as luxurious a notebook as you can afford and a pen you like to write with, and commit to writing down six things every evening. Jot down anything that has warmed your heart – a friendly smile on the bus, a picture drawn by one of your kids, an exciting new job, a walk on the beach, a warm house – and try to look for new things every day if you can. By the end of the month you'll have a bank of positive feelings and I guarantee you'll start to actively look for things to smile about, so you've got something to write in your journal! What's more, you're creating new reasons for the universe to reward you because our thoughts are magnetic and what we appreciate grows.

Create different perspectives

Another technique that really seems to work is one used by a dear friend of mine, Joey Walters, in her work with professional women's leadership groups. Joey's process originated through NLP (Neuro-linguistic Programming) and is based on the philosophy of Walt Disney, a gifted animator and businessman who used to turn up to his regular production meetings sporting a different persona each time. He would alternate at will between the Dreamer, the Critic and the Realist surprising his teams with his versatility and encouraging them all to do the same. Viewpoints from each individual's prevailing perspective were equally valued and included in the rigorous process of creation.

Joey uses this technique with spatial anchoring, writing the three states on individual pieces of paper and asking her delegates to really contact the feelings associated with each state as they physically stand on the relevant piece of paper. As thoughts come up they're asked to move between the pieces of paper and speak aloud the experience that comes from each state. There's also a meta-position where you can stand and view the whole integrated process and it helps to have a friend or coach nearby to prompt you if you get stuck. It's a surprisingly effective way to get in touch with your inner wisdom and unearth any fears, doubts or limiting beliefs.

Use your imagination

We have such a powerful tool at our disposal in the form of our imagination and most of the time we forget we even have it. Unless you follow your heart into acting or performing as an adult, 'play-acting' and pretending are only deemed acceptable when you're a child. By relegating this tool to our toy box as we move into adolescence we're abandoning one of the most valuable assets we have as adults.

Did you know that unless a child's imagination is developed through activities that encourage them to make mental pictures, for example story-telling and playing, their brains go through a myelination process, pruning the neural circuits they're not using and limiting their imaginations? Plonking them down in front of the TV doesn't help as it does all the work for them and their imaginations remain idle.

Our brains appear to be wired like computer circuits, with neural pathways processing information through the flow of electrochemical processes. Each neuron is like a living creature, however, extending tiny little arms and legs (axons and dendrites), which simultaneously interact with tens of thousands of other neurons. They're constantly talking to one another and they're constantly changing their connections to each other.

This quality of 'neuroplasticity' allows us to learn new skills and change poor behaviours. But we have to use them to strengthen them. The circuits that are activated most frequently will be strengthened while the unused neural circuits lose their power to influence our feelings, thoughts and behaviour. If we choose the right words, we'll prune away disruptive emotions and thought, streamlining the brain and making it more efficient. In the case of lost imagination, however, it could prove disastrous.

If repeatedly exposed to hostile, angry words the logical centre in the frontal cortex of the brain shuts down and over time repeated hostility can impair a child's ability to learn and predispose them to fearful, depressed thoughts. When language is violent it can cause havoc with the neurochemicals that shield us from stress. And these effects are not just limited to your moods, but will be experienced by your whole system.

Every cell in our body has memory as some people who've had organ transplants will testify. In her memoir, *A Change of Heart*, Claire Sylvia recounts a fascinating story, which will leave you in no doubt that our experiences can be embedded in our bodies. In 1988 Claire received a heart–lung transplant from an 18-year-old man who'd been killed in a motorcycle accident. As a former professional dancer Claire had been living a fairly fit and healthy life. Imagine her surprise when, after the transplant, she started craving fried chicken and beer, some of her donor's favourite indulgences!

There is plenty more evidence of cellular inheritance following organ transplants. One study conducted by Paul Pearsall PhD[2] reported incidences where recipients changed their sexual preferences, were suddenly able to play instruments, adopted some of the habits and talents of their donors and in some cases even relived the accidents that killed them.

In another recent study, a team led by Herbert Benson at Massachusetts General Hospital taught their subjects deep relaxation using diaphragmatic breathing and encouraged them to 'scan' their bodies for tension. Once they discovered an area of tension they were asked to repeat a single word or phrase that brought them peace or a sense of wellbeing. After eight weeks of practice, their subjects were able to alter up to 1,561 of their genes and significantly reduce their stress levels.

When we make a commitment to interrupting our negative thought processes and actively substituting positive language in our minds and in conversations with others, we can become more balanced and inject a little bit more peace into the world. But it's no good

---

2 Clark LV. Effect of mental practice on the development of a certain motor skill. *Research Quarterly*, v31 n4 (Dec 1960): 560–569

just engaging in positive thinking – we actually have to challenge the negative thoughts that arise and find out if they have any basis in truth or if they're sabotaging our happiness.

When I look around at the gloomy faces on the train, or listen to a catalogue of disasters on the news, it saddens me. Most of the time it seems that we've forgotten the magic of our existence. For a start, the very fact that one sperm made its way to an egg against all the odds of procreation is a miracle in itself. Or is miracle the right word? Little miracles become commonplace when we adopt the right frame of mind. We just have to be willing for them to start showing up in our lives and leave the rest to our imaginations.

The gateway to heaven is accessed through our consciousness and we can pass through it any time we like – we don't have to wait until we die. I think sometimes we forget that we are the only thinkers in our minds and we give away our power whenever we look outside ourselves for answers. If we all made a decision today to disbelieve all the strife and dis-ease that surrounds us and turn our thoughts, words and actions toward love, trust and truth, our worlds would transform overnight.

I've studied various religions over the years and always seem to get tripped up by dogma and exclusivity.

Rather than get caught up in discussions about which version is right or wrong I prefer to go out into nature and experience 'it' firsthand. Call 'it' God (or Good), enlightenment, Nirvana, whatever you wish – to me it's just the essence of pure love and it's equally accessible to everyone. My stepdaughter once told me in no uncertain terms that she absolutely did not believe in God. I responded 'That doesn't mean God doesn't believe in you. Do you believe in Love?'

'We-ll, yeah I s'pose' she replied.

To me they're the same.

If you can accept we're all spiritual beings having a human experience, I'm going to ask you to take one step further and imagine that our souls exist outside our bodies. Not locked up inside our mortal forms, waiting until we die, but continually surrounding us. And if thoughts magnetize matter, perhaps we are more capable than we realize of shaping our bodies and experiences. Why not? It's as plausible as all the other versions of reality we believe in. This would mean we really are all made of the same divine stuff. And instead of six billion separate souls there would be just one, in six billion different flavours! Baskin Robbins eat your heart out! ☺

4

TOOLS OF TRANSFORMATION

'Nothing is impossible; the word itself
says, "I'm possible"!'

Audrey Hepburn

'In the beginning was the Word, and
the Word was with God, and the Word
was God.'

The Bible, New Testament, John 1:1

'And whenever you give your word,
say the truth.'

The Koran, Surah al-An'am; 6:152

'Words have the power to both destroy
and heal. When words are both true
and kind, they can change our world.'

Buddhist saying

I love words. Ask anyone who knows me. Some would even say I speak in headlines. Shock, horror! Mellifluous, caress, cliffhanger, grockle ... how can you not be inspired? And moving to Scotland opened up a whole new vocabulary including 'cludgie' 'blether' and 'thunder-plump'.

The power of words to convey values and emotions, tell stories, connect us with people, causes and experiences is fascinating and I seem to have spent my career in the service of them. As Newspaper Sales Manager for a regional newspaper group in my late twenties, my job involved helping the editorial team choose the headlines for the day. We'd meet first thing in the morning and every afternoon to rank the stories in order of sales importance. Those headlines would then have to be distilled into no more than five attention-grabbing words and printed on a large poster for display outside news outlets.

A lot of research goes into the art of selling stories and the headlines you see are crafted to have the maximum impact with the minimum number of words. Fnords are words that instil fear or anxiety, for example 'horror', 'drama', 'attack', 'shock' and 'explosion' and are understood to be some of the most effective motivators when selling news stories or information.

Research gained from examining brain scans shows that there are two messages that cause the brain to light up in anticipation: threatening ones, and those that are filled with exaggerated positive claims. Unfortunately softer more abstract words don't tend to make such an impact ... unless they appeal to our 'lazy brain'. This is the pleasure centre of the brain that wants to take shortcuts, to achieve instant gratification without too much hard work. Ever bought a lottery ticket, responded to a 'get rich quick' scheme or signed up for a diet that promised to help you look like a supermodel without giving up the wine or chocolate? Then you've met your lazy brain!

Marketers are well versed in 'pushing our buttons', and finding the words, images and magic numbers, which will trigger us to act on these neurological impulses. Consider the 'explosion' (did your brain just light up?) of 12, seven and three-step programmes that have become so popular in books, blogs and on social media sites. You've only got to spend ten minutes on the internet to be presented with tips on how to do everything from 'burn 10lbs of belly fat' to 'earn six figures working from home'. Our brains must be lit up like Christmas trees during a typical browsing session!

Shape your reality

When I trained in the art of copywriting, we learned how to touch our readers' deepest emotions by writing text that appeals to a person's true values. In the wrong hands this skill could be used as a tool of manipulation, but I believe that coupled with an authentic intent it can weave magic.

Just look at the way words are used in the world to unite or divide. In the following telegram to General Alexander in 1942, Sir Winston Churchill managed to convey an entire military campaign in just 35 words:

'Your prime and main duty will be to take or destroy at the earliest opportunity the German–Italian army commanded by Field Marshal Rommel together with all its supplies and establishments in Egypt and Libya.'

In 1963 Martin Luther King influenced 250,000 people with his infamous 'I have a dream' speech (without the benefit of social media or a website) purely because of the strength of his beliefs and his ability to communicate them.

We speak of giving our word, keeping our word, choosing our words, living by our word. We use words to wound, to heal, to pray, to express, describe and to question. But it is not the actual words themselves that create consciousness or heal the body or change conditions. They're just the forms we use to express our feelings and thoughts. It is the awakened realizations behind them that have the real power, and words with spiritual power behind them must go forth and create.

We have the power to shape our reality using our thoughts, words and deeds. If we simply choose our thoughts and words with care, our actions will naturally follow and we will create what we think about. I say 'simply' but if you've ever tried to shepherd your thoughts or only speak with intent to heal, not harm – even for an hour – you'll realize it's quite a tall order. It takes practice and mindfulness while you create new neural pathways and allow old thought habits to drop away through non-use.

Let's look at it this way. Take a step back into the previous chapter and imagine that our souls exist outside our body, which is another way of saying that our spiritual essence is the surrounding, penetrating Love at the heart of all matter. This Love or universal intelligence is what animates our physical vessels. I believe that when we die we release our bodies into the dust and meld back into the essence of universal Love, perhaps picking up another body when we are ready.

Our physicists tell us that the world is made up of energy forms, which vibrate at different frequencies, with matter being the densest frequency. If this is so – and assuming that Spirit is the highest frequency – if we can raise our vibration to the level of Spirit, we can influence matter. It's not a case of forcing our thoughts into the spiritual realm; it's about letting go of our will and allowing our consciousness to merge with that higher state.

When we've contacted this elevated state we talk of being inspired, which derives from the Latin *inspirare*, meaning to breathe in. Sometimes meditation can take us to this place, but it can just as easily occur when we least expect it, when our minds are 'elsewhere'. All of a sudden an idea or solution might pop into our heads. We usually sense it's from a different source than the ideas or solutions we've laboured over in our minds before because the energy feels much newer and lighter. These inspirations are almost always accompanied by an 'aha moment', that feeling of 'why didn't I think of that before?' If we can imbue our words with this lighter energy, our words become inspirational and creative.

Thoughts are the next level of creation and magnetize matter. I firmly believe that whatever we think about, we are likely to become, and so it makes sense to raise your thought vibrations as high as possible and only concentrate on what you want to bring into being. You can usually tell the types of thoughts that most people over 40 have been habitually thinking, just by looking at their faces and postures. Angry people often have redder skin, while fear and worry can cause hair loss by contracting the scalp and squeezing the follicles to the extent that hair can't push through. Thoughts of pain and grief are always reflected in the body, and being judgmental or critical can often show up as arthritis and swollen joints. Kind, loving thoughts, however, create a kind of soft glow around a person, and a gentleness in the eyes.

Choose your thoughts

Regardless of what's going on around us, our thoughts are completely under our control. You might think 'that's just how it is' but if you go back far enough you'll find the point in your life where you chose a certain limiting thought and invested it with the power of belief. Sometimes the thought was accepted as truth before you were even conscious of it. If your parents believed for example that 'life is hard' or 'heart disease runs in our family' and passed that thought onto you before your own consciousness was fully formed, the likelihood is you adopted the belief as your own. And there's a strong probability that you have spent a good portion of your life since then attracting experiences that *prove* this limiting belief!

As children we are particularly susceptible to others' belief systems, as we have not had a chance to form our own based on experience. We learn more before the age of six than at any other time in our lives, literally downloading information from our surroundings and carers as a survival mechanism. Our immature brains operate mostly in the theta state as children, a 'super-learning' mindset similar to the trance state we enter into during hypnosis and between sleeping and waking. When we're in this state time seems to slow down and our subconscious minds are much more receptive, which is why meditating, reframing our day or listening to self-hypnosis recordings just before we drop off to sleep or immediately on waking is so powerful.

The good news is that we get the chance to choose our thoughts every minute of every day. It doesn't matter what you've believed or experienced in the past, or how harshly you've been judged (by yourself or others). The present moment holds the power and you hold all the keys. What a relief!

I find the best way to address our limiting beliefs is to cultivate a sense of humour. Treat it like a bit of a game and come from the perspective that we're all making it up as we go along, then you can create your own rules. Above all make it fun, let gentleness and love be your guides and never, *ever* criticize yourself for anything. Never. Even if you've crashed the car, pigged out on chocolate, hurt someone you love or whatever else constitutes 'bad' in your world.

Criticism of yourself or others is the fastest route to depression. Our every action comes wrapped up in its own consequences, some further reaching than we can imagine, and the universal law of 'what we give out we get back' will naturally redress any imbalance without us piling guilt and condemnation on top. Remember your thoughts are creative and you will only attract more of the same if you criticize or complain, inwardly or outwardly. As Louise Hay is consistently reminding us, we need to learn to love ourselves unconditionally for our lives to work on every level.

Create your transformation

Affirmations are one of the most effective tools for transformation. They are positive, passionate statements made in the present tense and repeated whenever we want to create a new state of being or eliminate an old one. For example if we were suffering with a health condition and wanted to create better health we might start monitoring our negative thoughts about our health and replace them with 'I am healthy, healed and whole'. In this situation, as with any other where a sense of lack is present, it's vital to stop telling ourselves or other people about our negative condition. Talking about your poor health or lack of money can only keep those conditions in your life – remember you are a powerful creative being! Instead, every time a thought arises about your health, use your affirmations to redirect your thoughts.

'I am' statements are the most powerful of all because 'I am' is the creative principle. The 'I' is the masculine part, the declaration of your true spiritual identity, while the 'am' represents the feminine quality, which brings into being whatever it conceives or embraces. The two words together embody the complete creative process and if spoken or thought with a high spiritual intention will bring into being whatever follows them. Interestingly the Hindu equivalent is 'aum' (also known as 'om') which translates literally as 'Yes' or 'It is' and is thought to be the original vibratory tone of the universe.

It's easy to get caught up in whatever we're experiencing in the world and it takes discipline to turn our thoughts to the spiritual realm and manifest the ideals that are available to us all. Poor health, abusive relationships, poverty and hardship are all too 'real' when they become an accepted feature of our lives. The hardest thing for me to accept, when I was hovering on the brink of bankruptcy or almost bleeding to death each month, was the part I was playing in creating these conditions. When someone tells you that to change your world all you have to do is change your thoughts and words, it's almost as insulting as a slap in the face. The ego is outraged at such a preposterous and overly simplistic solution! It starts throwing its full weight behind defending its position and chucking out all kinds of accusations and justifications. Blah, blah, blah. A truly Oscar-winning performance ... and you're guaranteed a front-row seat!

If we get stuck at this point we'll continue to reproduce all the same old patterns until we find another temporary 'miracle cure', which might absolve us of the responsibility of looking directly at the underlying cause of our problems for a little while longer. But true long-term relief can only come from taking full responsibility and getting right to the heart of the matter.

How often have you pointed the finger and projected a problem 'out there' onto someone or something else? If you're like me, and most of the people I know, it'll be hundreds, possibly thousands of times. Notice when you physically point, how many more fingers on your hand are pointing back in your direction? Yep. There's only one place you can start if you really want your life to change.

An affirmation is actually anything we say or think. The world of matter is responding to the creative energy behind every thought we have and every word we speak. The first time I learned this and took it to heart was during my training as a 'Heal Your Life' teacher and I can tell you it shook me to my core. As well as the responsibility that it carried, the sheer effort of policing all my thoughts and words shocked me into virtual silence for about a week! It also made me realize just how much of our self-talk and conversations are negative. Maybe it's a British quirk but we have a tendency to start a lot of our dialogues with a moan or a gossip. The weather, the traffic, the government and other people – nothing's safe from an occasional slating!

Returning to the vibrational theme, if each positive thought or intention resonates at a high frequency and attracts matter of the same vibrational density, the same must be true of negative thoughts and words at the opposite end of the spectrum. Surely spending our time and energy on thoughts and words that can only attract experiences we don't want is a wasted opportunity?

Positive words foster growth

I like a good moan like anyone else – it's great for letting off steam and, let's face it, some of our best humour can be drawn from the days when the world seems to be plotting against us – but when I want to create beauty and harmony around and within myself I choose my words and thoughts with care. Mantras and affirmations are two of the most effective ways to change our thoughts and experiences.

The latest neurological research reveals that by choosing our words and thoughts with care and concentrating on them specifically for ten to 20 minutes every day, we can actually change the functioning in key areas of our brain by as much as 25 per cent. For example, simply by focusing on a word such as 'peace' you will begin to feel peaceful and the emotional centres in your brain will start to calm down.

In their groundbreaking book, *Words Can Change Your Brain*, neuroscientists Andrew Newberg and Mark Robert Waldman explain that once your parietal and frontal lobes have been stimulated by the positive word or thought you're holding in your mind, the message will be relayed by the thalamus to other parts of your brain, effectively slowing down the limbic system's ability to generate neurochemical messages of anxiety, irritability or depression. This sets up a self-reinforcing pattern in our brains. The frontal lobe includes specific language centres, which are directly connected to the motor cortex responsible for moving us into action and therefore influencing behaviour. As these language centres are stimulated by our peaceful feelings, we are more likely to act in a calmer way, which generates more serene thoughts and strengthens the new neural circuits being created and so the cycle continues. Words can even alter the expression of genes throughout the brain and body, turning them on and off and thereby changing the way we biologically grow.

After just a few weeks of repetitive practice you'll begin to change your brain positively. In fact – as one new study found – even looking at a list of positive words for just a few seconds will improve the mood of an anxious or depressed person. Try this every day for a month. Write out a list of words that have a very positive connotation for you, meditate on them for ten minutes every morning and ten minutes before you go to bed and note how your mood changes.

Our brains, however, are even more sensitively attuned to negative communication, particularly the word 'no', and if you stare at a list of negative words, you'll immediately feel worse. As soon as your amygdala – an almond-shaped fight or flight button that rests in the centre of your primitive emotional brain – interacts with a negative word or phrase, stress-producing hormones and neurotransmitters are released, interfering with the functioning of your whole body and mental processes. Memory and emotions are particularly affected and research suggests that the more we focus on negative feelings and thoughts, the more likely we are to damage key structures of our emotional limbic system, leading to disruptions in sleep patterns, appetite, moods and the way our brain regulates happiness, longevity and health. Ruminating on negative thoughts about the past or future predisposes us to unhappiness and even clinical depression.

Worse still, if you broadcast your negativity or listen to someone else's, even more stress chemicals will be released into your system, putting you at risk of increased irritability, anxiety and depression. One more reason not to watch the news before bedtime!

According to the latest research, the fastest way to convert negative or fearful thoughts into positive feelings is to adopt an optimistic, relaxed approach to problems and goals. As our attitudes are really just a string of words, thoughts, images and feelings, consciously editing and directing these inputs creates new neural circuits that can easily communicate the reformed message to other areas of the brain.

If you've tried using affirmations before without much success I can only encourage you to try again. If you're affirming for something – let's say relief from a health condition – and nothing's happening, the likelihood is you'll be having what I call a five-to-one experience. Your lips might be moving, the words may be coming out but for every positive statement you are making, there'll be five negative thoughts lurking behind your mental bushes waiting to ambush it. The poor little affirmation hasn't got a hope of surviving in such a climate of fear and discontent. Here's an example (thoughts in italics):

'I am healthy, healed and strong.'

Don't feel very healthy. Maybe I'll never be healed. Mum had this for years and she never found a cure, so I'm bound to be stuck with it, too. This whole process is ridiculous. Why did I ever think it could work? Better go back to the doctor/take a pill/look it up on Google. At least I know where I am with that.

All these are just distractions, ways of resisting true change. Affirmations are meant to be statements of intent – something you want to bring into being – rather than reflections of the situation you find yourself in when you start using them. Rather than see positive affirmations as escapist fantasies or unrealistic expectations, try to see them as little seeds of hope for the future. It's your job to protect these little seedlings from the frost of your cynicism, to shelter and nurture them until they're strong and rooted enough to stand on their own.

Tending your thoughts takes time, complete honesty and patience. When you first start listening to your internal conversation and monitoring your thoughts and words it's like working with a tangled ball of wool and just finding an end to grab hold of can be quite a challenge. But please, please keep at it – the results are definitely worthwhile.

Once you've decided on an affirmation that feels right for you, for example 'I am healthy, happy and free', the first question to ask yourself is 'how will my life change if this affirmation comes true?' If you can remain completely open when you ask this question, the answers might surprise you. Of course there'll be gains – better health, more energy, a feeling of achievement, etc. – but there might be some losses, too. Perhaps you worry that no one will take care of you if you're completely well. Maybe you'll have to work more hours. Sometimes you'll need to take responsibility for imbalances in your relationships. These are some of the 'icky' issues that underpin your resistance and no doubt you'll discover your own versions. They usually have their roots in fear or feelings of unworthiness and they're often incredibly uncomfortable to face head-on. But face them we must if we are to get to the bottom of the 'situation' we want to change.

I once spent several days dancing around an issue that was bothering me. My right shoulder was giving me trouble and there seemed to be a blockage in the blood flow to my right hand. I tried affirmations, stretching, massage, acupuncture and everything in-between without much success. In fact the problem just kept getting worse and worse until eventually my nails were starting to turn blue and my fingers had swollen so much I couldn't use a keyboard or hold a pen. I asked myself how my life might change if my arm was healed and it was then that the penny dropped. If I couldn't type or hold a pen I couldn't write this book. And if I couldn't write this book I wouldn't be opening myself to ridicule. The whole situation was based on an old fear of which I hadn't even been consciously aware. Within an hour of releasing that fear using the 'heart of the matter' process, my shoulder, arm and hand had completely returned to normal. Our thoughts are so powerful.

Forgiveness

If you find you're still stuck after answering this question, it usually means there's some forgiveness work to be completed. Forgiveness is a tricky concept and often gets muddled up with reconciliation. When we forgive, it's an act of self-love: a way to free ourselves from negativity and reclaim our power. We don't even need to communicate with the person we're forgiving; yet they'll probably feel the release on an energetic level. Forgiving someone does not mean we are condoning their behaviour or allowing it to continue. Sometimes the most loving action is to set a boundary and stick to it. It does however mean we're releasing the person, seeing past their pain and limitations to the divine being within. After all, we are all one.

Forgiveness shines a light into the dark recesses of history. Nelson Mandela's capacity for forgiveness allowed the South African nation to move forward and I clearly remember being moved to tears when I heard a radio interview with Enniskillen survivor Gordon Wilson. Gordon lay underneath the rubble caused by the Remembrance Day bombing in November 1987, holding his daughter's hand as she died. He recalled their final conversation:

'She held my hand tightly, and gripped me as hard as she could and she said, "Daddy, I love you very much." Those were her exact words to me, and those were the last words I ever heard her say.'

Astonishingly, Wilson continued, 'But I bear no ill will. I bear no grudge. Dirty sort of talk is not going to bring her back to life. She was a great wee lassie. She loved her profession. She was a pet. She's dead. She's in heaven and we shall meet again. I will pray for these men tonight and every night.'

Gordon Wilson went on to become a campaigner for peace. The effect of his forgiveness was felt around the world and as historian Jonathan Bardon recounts, 'No words in more than twenty-five years of violence in Northern Ireland had such a powerful, emotional impact.'

Perhaps one of the most inspirational stories of forgiveness comes from author Joe Vitale who introduces Dr Ihaleakala Hew Len and the Huna practice of Ho'o pono pono to us. Dr Len is a psychologist in Hawaii who used this practice to cure a whole ward of criminally insane patients ... without ever seeing any of them.

As he studied each inmate's chart he looked deep within himself to discover how he had created that person's dis-ease. Read that again if you have to. How *he* had created that person's disease. As the doctor healed *himself*, the patients improved and eventually every one of them was released and the ward was closed. This takes self-responsibility to a whole new level. It also adds weight to the theory that we are all one.

It would suggest that anything that exists within your life is your responsibility, a projection of what's inside you. To heal your world you need to love every bit of yourself, good and bad, dark and light. If you don't like the state of the economy, heal your money issues. If your relationships don't work, get to work on your self-love.

The technique used by Dr Len was very simple and I urge you to try it yourself. As he reviewed each patient's file he would repeat 'I'm sorry', and 'I love you', over and over again. It doesn't have to be difficult. If you're holding onto a situation or blaming another – or yourself – visualize that person and repeat these two phrases until you feel the energy free itself. It really works.

You'll know when you've forgiven yourself or someone else because the difficulties you were facing will magically resolve themselves. It can be instantaneous or may take a few 'sleeps' (as my six-year-old niece calls them) to let go. Often all it takes is your willingness. If you direct yourself to that inner space where you can find even a tiny spark of willingness to forgive, the universe will take care of the details. Sometimes a kind of amnesia can set in at this point – it's as if we've forgotten we even had the problem until something or someone causes us to notice it's no longer a feature of our lives.

Don't be afraid to let go of your affirmations when you've outgrown them. They're only meant to be stepping-stones to success. When you've got to where you wanted to be when you set out, it's time to dream up some more!

Tune in to the universe

Although I trust in the potency of words and thoughts, I think the real authority lies in silence and intent. Dr Masaru Emoto's famous rice experiment demonstrated the power of our thoughts, words and – perhaps most importantly – intent on matter. In this experiment, Dr Emoto sealed some boiled rice in three jars. During the experiment, only pleasant words were directed at the first jar, which also bore a label saying 'Thank You'. Conversely, only harsh words were spoken to and written on the second jar. The third jar or 'control' was set aside and completely ignored. After one month, the rice in the first 'positive' jar had started to ferment, giving off a pleasant odour. Rice in the second 'negative' jar had turned black. But here's where it starts to get interesting because the rice in the third 'ignored' jar was rotten and mouldy.

Much has been made of the implications of this experiment relating to the power of positive thinking. I'm more intrigued, however, by the results in the third jar. It would seem that *any* attention is better than none, as proven by the research of Dr Rene Spitz in 1945, where he observed the fate of 34 infants in a foundling home who were deprived of maternal love and affection. In total 27 babies died in their first year and a further seven in their second year. Giving no attention to a person or animal that is dependent on you can obviously have detrimental effects. However, removing our attention from a condition may lead it to fall into decay faster. Surely this adds weight to the theory that 'energy flows where attention goes', and could be used to beneficial effect if we're trying to eliminate a negative condition or manifest a positive state in our lives?

The universe's mighty power resides within us all and when we take the time to be still and align ourselves with it, our beings become harmonized. Being silent is an instant shortcut to harmony because, by stilling the mind and seeking unity, you raise your body's vibration to a state where strife cannot exist. Discord only prevails at the mortal level.

According to the Oxford English Dictionary, the original meaning of the Greek word 'chaos' was 'the formless matter supposed to have existed before the creation of the universe'. Rather than being a synonym for disorder, the original meaning had more in common with the Eastern Tao.

When we connect with this 'formless matter' and align our intent with that of Universal Love through silence and unity, we are imbued with the power to bring forth perfection. Many of the world's eminent artists, musicians, scientists, philosophers and healers have expressed this quality through their work and I'm sure there have been many moments in your life when you have, too.

If you have trouble accepting that you are part of divine consciousness and have the tools of creation to hand, try affirming 'I am one with divine perfection', before you go to sleep at night. In sleep we rejoin universal consciousness where anything's possible. Suspend all your disbelief and in those moments before sleep become like a child again, enchanted by your favourite fairytale. After all, nobody else need know what you're thinking. The power of your imagination will go to work while you sleep, transforming your dreams into reality. At the very least, your dreams will be magical ...

5

FINDING YOUR PURPOSE

'Nothing is work unless you'd rather
be doing something else.'

George Halas

What would you most love to do right now? How would you like to earn money? What can you offer to the world? OK, the temptation might be to say 'I'd love to be sitting on a beach in the Seychelles enjoying my lottery winnings', but taking the long-term view, you probably have some idea of a special way you'd like to contribute.

Everyone believes that his or her ideal job is out there somewhere. But most of the time we'll stop ourselves from getting it because of our inner beliefs. This is usually because we don't think we're worthy of our dream job; we need more qualifications, skills, charisma, youth, energy, experience, people skills, opportunities ... the list goes on. For years my low self-esteem made sure I talked myself out of every prospect going, and this was despite having already been 'successful' in the eyes of the world.

Even if we dare to believe it's possible, we can trip ourselves up by concentrating on what we don't want rather than visualizing the dream we are hoping to attract. Passion doesn't exist in the job; it resides within us. If we're mooching around at work saying to ourselves 'I really don't want this job. It's dull, the pay's lousy and I can't stand my boss', the universe is going to respond with 'That's right.'

For anything to change, we must be able to ignite

that excitement and gratitude within ourselves right now wherever we are. Once you tap into that, the universe will start to restructure itself around your dreams faster than you can imagine.

So give some thought to what type of work would really make your heart sing. What unique skills do you have? Trust me, you'll discover some. Ask your friends and family what they appreciate in you. Take yourself back to being a kid and remember what interested you then. Imagine that the world is conspiring **with** you to achieve your dreams, and see every footfall along the way as a step in the right direction.

When you have a crystal-clear, full-colour picture of your dream in your mind and can intuit the feelings you'll have once you've achieved it, start picturing yourself living in it. Imagine a day in the life of the new you; the kind of clothes you'll wear, the hours you'll work, the lifestyle you'll have. It takes a surprising amount of time to really define what you want but it's worth sticking with it, as this is the hardest part. And you can keep refining it as you go. The important thing is to keep it fun, approach it with a curious, light-hearted attitude and dare to believe.

Now every time you catch yourself thinking 'I don't want this job,' just imagine your new picture and switch the thought to 'I love my new life! I'm delighted to be earning (insert figure) doing work that fulfils and inspires me.' Feel free to change the words to suit you, but do make sure your affirmations are positive, in the present tense and feature emotive words like 'love', 'excite', 'delight' and 'inspire'. This is bound to feel false for a while but if you're willing to suspend your disbelief and persevere, you will start to feel lighter and opportunities will seem to come from nowhere.

Appreciate now to change the future

The fastest way to effect change is to start genuinely appreciating what you have right now, while envisaging your future reality as if you're already in it. So if you want a new job or career, start to notice everything about your current job or situation that brings you pleasure. It could just be a regular income, free time, a warm office, happy customers, friendly colleagues ... whatever – just be appreciative. Take the time to develop an authentic interest in the people around you, regardless of how they behave toward you. They'll change before your eyes.

By this stage, you might be thinking your situation isn't all that bad, but if you still want to leave, imagine your job going to someone who'll really appreciate it and see the transition happening smoothly.

I've practised this technique many times, both on myself and with friends, and the only thing that continues to surprise is the speed at which change manifests if we're wholehearted in our approach ... and how much resistance to it we can still create! For example, during a weekend workshop, one lady envisaged her dream cottage, right down to the last detail. She also saw herself embracing her ideal career and earning a full-time wage working just two days a week. Within just one week, she had masterfully manifested the whole scenario, but managed to talk herself out of it because she didn't feel ready! Happily, she recognized what had happened and took more gradual steps toward her dream.

Having struggled with my equilibrium and associated health problems for two years (there was a hidden belief system here around having to work at a 'proper job', which stopped me from doing it sooner), I started re-visioning my ideal work/life balance. (The very fact that we put 'work' before 'life' in this statement shows me how out of balance we have become as a society.) Surely in an ideal world, our work would be an outer expression of who we are as people? Let's really go out on a limb and propose that the whole purpose of education should be to explore a developing person's strengths and encourage them to nurture their natural talents. Anyway, I took a long, hard look at this equation and decided that I would like to split my time between my healing practice, writing (commercially and for fun) and working for a children's charity.

And that's exactly what I do.

The best of all we can be

I'm very lucky to have had two loving, supportive parents. My dad is a rock, a tower of strength for all his dependents. He works incredibly hard, is scrupulously honest and is careful to use his word honourably. No matter how badly someone lets him down, you rarely hear him use blame. He's more likely to put himself in the other person's shoes and try to understand the situation from their perspective. He's a true provider and a natural leader.

Mum is the softer one: she's all about love and nurture. Bright and bubbly, she'll have you laughing in moments and shows her love by her optimism and understanding. She always has another way of looking at things and really knows how to care for people.

So the messages I grew up with were 'you are safe and you are loved'. I believe these are two of the most important messages you can give anyone. It took me 40 years to accept their gifts and although my folks are as human and fallible as the rest of us, I am eternally grateful for their legacy.

I believe this is how evolution happens. Our jobs, as human beings, are to be the best of all we can be, which requires us to synthesize the gifts we receive from our parents and express them in a new way, which is uniquely ours. This way, the best of the generations survive and flourish through our children. I don't think this is limited to genetic parents either – anyone who has been exposed to the qualities of influential adults on a regular basis will have these qualities as part of their toolkit, too. So grandparents, family friends, stepfamilies, neighbours and teachers all have their part to play.

Look to see who influenced your early years. What message did they have for you? You may well find that if you look for the positive, and recognize that they were only human and were doing the best job they could, the message they gave you helped your evolution, and tied in well with what you know to be your purpose in the world. Because we do all know that.

Ask any child what they're good at and they will tell you. Maybe it doesn't fit into any recognized career path or job description, but most of us know from a young age why we're here. My family recall my uncle once asking me what I was going to do when I grew up.

I drew myself up to my full six-year-old height, took a deep breath and fixed him with a very serious look. 'I'm going to help people feel better', I pronounced.

It's important to ask these questions, not just once but throughout our lives. Few of us in the twenty-first century will stick with one job or even one career path throughout our working lifetimes. Whereas in the past it was seen as a positive trait and evidence of your 'stickability' to stay with one organization and work your way up through its ranks, it can now be viewed as lacking aspiration.

With home working, freelancing, flexi-time, sabbaticals, family friendly policies and advances in technology, there is now more scope than ever before to create a flexible working structure that suits you. 'Portfolio incomes' are becoming more and more common.

Think about the unconscious messages you received about work while you were growing up. Did you observe your parents working at professions they loved, or was work considered a 'necessary evil'? Perhaps you grew up in a single-parent family or a household where one or both parents were unemployed? Maybe there was resentment around being a houseparent or full-time carer? Regardless of the actual experience, it's the feelings and undercurrents that you would have picked up on as a child.

My journey

Like many women in the 1980s I became a victim of
my success trying to be a man in the world of work.
Throughout my childhood, my father, a self-made
entrepreneur, would impress me with his business
acumen, his ability to 'deal' with things and make
things happen. My mother, in contrast, appeared more
emotional and indecisive. I gave little thought to who
provided my daily infrastructure – the meals, the hugs,
the cosy chats and little comforts; for me, the world only
turned Technicolor when he walked in the door.

I see now that without Mum's loving support, given
willingly but with the sacrifice of a lot of her personal
freedom, Dad wouldn't have been empowered to achieve
a fraction of what he has in the world. It was Mum that
nursed him when at 25 he contracted a stress-related
stomach ulcer, which made him physically sick every
day for five years. She who counselled him when things
weren't going so well and encouraged him to take risks
he may not have dared to take alone. She he turned to
for a balanced perspective, and she and her own mother
who jollied us all along to reach our full potential.

But no, none of that registered in my 12-year-old
heart. That emotional stuff just kept the pilot light
going, it was never going to set the world on fire. For

true success you needed balls, the bigger the better! And I was gonna grow some!

While I was at grammar school, Margaret Thatcher was elected. The country watched with interest to see how a government would fare with a woman at the helm. Would she rule with intuition, benevolence and a fair hand? Or would she tap into her darker forces and summon manipulation, divisiveness and malevolence?

Time tells its own story, but back then it seemed that her arrival on the scene opened up many previously closed doors for emerging young women. Choices lit up our career paths. Would we become doctors, scientists, lawyers? Set up homes or a business? Few could truly advise us, as this was mostly uncharted territory. My own and most of my friends' middle-class mothers had spent a lot of their adult lives supporting husbands and families or worthy causes. There were a few exceptions – my best friend's mum ran a very successful hairdressing salon and another was an hotelier – but they were in the minority.

Careers guidance relied on a computer, which matched your skills and interests with a career path. My choices were a journalist or a jeweller. My husband Seth tells me he was advised to become a potter, but then he's always been very in touch with his feminine side!

So there we were, fledgling businesswomen, prepared to take the world by storm. We had the education, the confidence, the enthusiasm and the energy, but we were missing one vital tool. A penis.

The one thing everyone had neglected to tell us was that if we wanted a piece of the action we were going to have to become like men to get it. Hierarchies were not built on stilettos.

The world was not yet ready to accept the full might of our feminine power. So we were allowed into the office but not the boardroom. If we proved that we could play the game according to the rules, we might even be given a position of (limited) authority.

I joined the newspaper industry and was fortunate to have some enlightened male bosses who were prepared to give me a chance. At the tender age of 25 I was promoted from a junior to a senior position. Overnight I went from being a telesales representative to a senior manager running a sales department, largely staffed by middle-aged men who had been with the company for at least 20 years and weren't about to be bossed around by a young whippersnapper – especially not a woman! It was a baptism of fire and I made it my mission to 'beat the boys at their own game'.

Five years later I was completely burned out, my first marriage was in tatters and I could hardly face the mask that stared dispassionately back at me from the mirror. Like Jim Carrey in the film *The Mask*, I had become the role and lost myself in the process. I have since met far too many women who have followed the same path. On the day I realized this I resigned and vowed never to put myself in that situation again.

I was very lucky to have received some of the best leadership training money could buy during my time in newspapers. I wish, however, I'd had access to some of the 'self-leadership' tools I've learned since – it would have made life a lot easier.

Thankfully, the world is shifting, and many more women are successfully combining careers with family life and interests, without losing themselves in the process. As our consciousness becomes more balanced and people feel more comfortable drawing equally on their yin (feminine/receptive) and yang (masculine/active) qualities, our working lives will be enriched in ways we've yet to see unfold.

Starting afresh

When you have stopped enjoying what you're doing, it's a sign that something new is needed in your life. It could be a new job, a different direction or a change of attitude, but you'll probably recognize it first as a vague feeling of dissatisfaction. You might brush it aside or pretend it doesn't exist, particularly if the prospect of altering course scares you. But change doesn't need to cause anxiety – in reality it's the only constant companion you'll have throughout your life. If it's time to make changes and you cling to your 'old' ways of doing things, you may find your soul gives a helping hand and will start creating circumstances where the 'old ways' no longer work.

Redundancy is a case in point. The thought that you could lose your job and have to let go of a lot of the familiar routines your 'lazy brain' has become accustomed to, fills most people with terror. It's usually accompanied by the prospect of losing income too, so it's easy to spiral into fear and abandon our self-nurturing practices. Yet if we can keep the boat steady and plot a course through it by connecting more often with our inner wisdom using meditation and introspection, redundancy can be a catalyst for us to re-evaluate our lives and follow our dreams. Start your own business, go freelance, travel or retrain – you just need to commit to take the first step, remember?

The best affirmations to use in this situation are the ones that relinquish control. After all, your soul has brought you this experience because it sees a better way. So use 'I let go easily, trusting that nothing leaves my life unless something better is coming'. Trust that you will be guided to take the right action at the appropriate time. And if well-meaning friends, colleagues or family members try to sabotage that trust and quiet confidence by drawing you into fearful scenarios, gently disengage from the conversation and bring yourself back to your centre. If you only use positive language when talking to people about your working life, you'll also be showing them a new way to allay their fears, which will open up fresh opportunities for them too. Remember that the event doesn't control your future – you do!

If you're in a challenging work environment, there are many things you can do to effect change, even in seemingly rigid situations. Take the time to sit with your ideal situation and send love to every atom of it. Remember, part of bringing our dreams into reality involves fully accepting and being grateful for where we're at right now. Try not to focus on the negatives. Instead, start acting as if you'd already achieved whatever you wanted to bring into being at work. If that means getting a better position, use affirmations such as 'I love my new job', but make sure you also love your current job. It seems counter-intuitive, I know, but it's the fastest route to changing your circumstances.

The quickest path to misery is to take a job you don't enjoy, whether it's well paid or not. In an economic recession when jobs are scarce and unemployment is high it may be difficult to see that you still have choices and you might begin to feel trapped. Sometimes that can be an excuse for not taking responsibility for our lives, but if you're clear that you're ready for change and make the effort to find something positive about your situation I guarantee it will improve. Over the years I've had all sorts of jobs that I didn't think were in alignment with my true purpose – domestic care in a retirement home, serving hospital meals, endless typing jobs for less than the minimum wage, even dressing up as a chicken to sell chocolate eggs! – but each one taught me something. I've also launched a successful business in the middle of a recession, so that's another myth busted.

If you run your own business, you obviously have much more control over your working practices and environment. Use this opportunity to bring heaven down to earth and create a company that can really make a difference, just by its attitude. Change your words to change your world and nurture every single person with whom you come into contact. Cherish every customer and colleague. In my copywriting business, Purplefeather, we use affirmations regularly – to birth our mission statement and core values and to set our intentions for the working week. Instead of strategy and sales meetings, get to the heart of what you want to achieve on a daily basis and visualize it happening. If you work with others, get them involved, too – shared visualization is extremely powerful.

Your work should be an expression of your love in the world. If you truly love what you do it shows. Working for yourself gives you a golden chance to set the framework for that expression. If you bake pies, put love and care into every one – they'll taste so much better! If you're a lawyer, offer everyone dignity and respect. If you're in sales or services, go the extra mile for your customers and treat their need as if it were your own. Not just because it's the 'right' thing to do, but also because it's a true expression of who you really are – love embodied.

This is truly living your life's purpose. All it takes is a bit of courage and the willingness to go inside and listen to your heart's desires. You'll wonder why you didn't try it years ago.

What do you choose?

I'd like to finish this chapter with a story I once read about an inspirational restaurateur whose attitude sums up how important it is to recognize that we always have choices.

Jerry was one of those guys you love to hate – always positive and cheerful, never in a bad mood. Whenever he was asked how he was doing, his response would always be the same: 'If I were any better I'd be twins!'

As the manager of a successful restaurant he was responsible for a large team and his waiting staff always seemed happy and motivated. When asked about his motivational style he replied 'It's simple. Every morning I wake up and say to myself "OK Jerry, you've got two choices today. You can choose to be in a good mood or a bad mood." Every time something bad happens I can choose to be a victim or I can choose to learn from it. If someone complains to me I can choose to accept their complaint or help them see a more positive side of life. I am the only one who can decide how I respond – and I choose the positive every time.'

One morning Jerry made a mistake. He left the back door of the restaurant open and was held up at gunpoint by three armed robbers. As he tried to open the safe, his hand started to shake and slipped off the combination. The robbers panicked and shot him. Jerry was fortunate to be found quickly and rushed to hospital and after 18 hours of surgery and weeks in intensive care he was sent home with fragments of the bullets still in his body. When asked how he was doing, his response was slightly different: 'If I were any better I'd be twins! Wanna see my scars?'

Some months later he was asked what had gone through his mind during the robbery.

'My first thought was that I should have locked the back door. Then when I was lying on the floor I realized I still had a choice – to live or die. I chose to live. The paramedics were great, constantly telling me I was going to be OK, but when I was wheeled into the emergency room and saw the expressions on the faces of the medics, I got pretty scared. They had already decided I was a dead man. I knew I needed to take action so when a big burly nurse asked if I was allergic to anything I took a deep breath and yelled, "Yes!" Everyone stopped working. "Bullets!" When they'd stopped laughing I told them "I am choosing to live. Operate on me as if I'm alive, not dead".'

Jerry survived, not only because of the skill of his doctors, but also because of his attitude. You always have choices and the greatest gift you give others is an example of your life working. Follow your dreams and never believe you have all the answers. You'll be amazed where you end up!

6

TRANSFORMING RELATIONSHIPS

'Forgiveness is the fragrance that
the violet sheds on the heel that has
crushed it.'

Mark Twain

We are in relationship with everything and everyone we come into contact with. I have a relationship with my husband, my stepdaughters, my family and friends, the dog, my desk, the sky, the trees, my colleagues, the lady who works on the checkout in my local supermarket and, of course, all the people who I may not meet on a daily basis who are an intrinsic part of my life. The bus drivers, energy suppliers, farmers, bankers, employers, retailers ... you get the picture. It's so easy to forget that we're all inter-connected.

In her inspirational book *Creative Visualisation*, Shakti Gawain says:

'The people we are in relationships with are always a mirror reflecting our own beliefs, and simultaneously we are mirrors, reflecting their beliefs. A relationship with another human being is one of the most powerful tools for growth that we have; if we look honestly at our relationships we can see so much about how we have created them.'

Thomas à Kempis in his book *The Imitation of Christ* urges us to 'seek to overcome that in ourselves which most disturbs us in other people.'

Both these statements turn our usual preconceptions about relationships on their head and places accountability for them firmly at our doorstep.

One of my favourite quotes is:

'God grant me the serenity to accept the people I cannot change, the courage to change the one I can, and the wisdom to know it's me.'

Getting to the heart of the matter in relationships requires us to be completely objective, which can be extremely difficult when our deepest feelings are involved. We need to assume total responsibility for every facet of how they work, or don't. If they are difficult, look to see what makes them so. Where are you not getting your needs met? What is making you unhappy? Then examine how you've been contributing to the problem and how you're benefiting from keeping yourself miserable. There is a need for every 'situation' we have in our lives, otherwise we wouldn't be creating it. What would happen if you let go of the need for the discontent in your relationships?

Very often when we start delving into our closest connections with other people we come up against some primal emotions such as fear, anger, mistrust, jealousy, disdain and guilt. We modelled our earliest relationships on our families and many of us carry our unresolved issues with us into adulthood. If we had a critical father, chances are we will still be looking for approval from our partners. Sibling rivalry will spill over into friendships and we may unconsciously repeat parenting patterns with our own children.

Relationship expert Sondra Roy asserts that we will keep attracting relationships that mirror our interactions with our parents until we are ready to heal any issues surrounding that primary bond. We might save ourselves an awful lot of time if we decide to do that today.

Forgive people and the past

Neither people nor your past need to have a hold over you. This is not about condoning hurtful behaviour, just not holding onto the thorns of it. *A Course in Miracles* describes forgiveness as removing a block from our awareness of love's presence. It's surprising how much energy is released when we forgive. Equally important is forgiving yourself for past mistakes. Even if you perceive you did something 'unforgivable' remember that you, like everyone else, were just doing the best you could at the time.

If you can put aside some time for yourself where you're not likely to be disturbed, try writing your relationship autobiography. Start with your closest family, move on to your earliest friends, schoolmates and extended family. Then expand into your network of adult relationships, friendships and colleagues. Perhaps your partner's family comes next and maybe your children and grandchildren. Look at the inter-connections between yourself and all these people. How did they come into your life? How do they make you feel? What are the strengths and weaknesses within your relationships? Where are the flashpoints, the harmonies? How many are mirrors of your primary relationships with parents or guardians?

Chances are you won't have gone through your life so far without hurting or being hurt by someone – it's all part of our growth. While you're writing your autobiography, make a separate list of anyone who's ever hurt or disappointed you with a note of what they did or said. Include yourself if you feel you let yourself down. Visualize sitting opposite each one of these people, having a conversation about how you feel. When you've expressed any negative feelings and are ready to let go of the emotion, (this might take some time) say you're sorry and you love them and imagine releasing the whole situation heavenward. When you reach the end of your list, write across it 'I am willing to forgive and let go', then shred or burn the list. Most people find that by this time they're feeling considerably lighter and calmer.

With those closest to you it might take more than one exercise to complete the forgiveness but the payback will be worth it, as they'll also feel the release on an energetic level. Roberto Assagioli once said 'When joy is present, war is impossible.' Think about this being true inside the body as well as outside.

To experience joy, you have to be present for it – you have to be awake and aware in all your senses in the present moment, not preoccupied with what's happened or what's going to happen. This is not the way we usually live so it can take practice, but learning how to be present to yourself is an essential part of healing. You have to have unhooked yourself from the past and the future before you can be present enough to know what is going on in your relationships.

Sometimes when I'm out walking in nature, I remind myself to stop. Because I often work from home, I take regular breaks outdoors and most of the time my mind is chewing away on some imagined problem. On enlightened days I'll remember to stop and sit or lean against a tree, tasting the air, drinking in the birdsong. It helps pull me into the present where all the solutions are to be found. Captivated by the sights, sounds and smells of my surroundings, I'll momentarily loosen my grip on my mind's concerns and by the time I come back to them they've usually solved themselves. Or I'll come back to my computer refreshed to find a message from someone who can help. Miracles happen every day!

Another way to bring your awareness into the present is through mindfulness: paying attention on purpose and without judgment. Multi-tasking can add to stress, whereas pouring your attention into one task at a time can soothe the mind and enhance the senses.

When you adopt this non-judgmental attitude toward yourself and others, it frees up all kinds of relationships and people will start showing their best qualities to you. Even when they don't, if you continue to silently beam goodwill towards them and treat them with loving kindness, they'll have a hard time hanging on to their poor behaviour for very long.

Act as if...

If you catch yourself indulging in negative thinking, either about yourself or other people, act as if you're directing internal traffic and stop the thought in its tracks. Now think of its opposite, make sure it's in the present tense and infuse it with as much passion as you can muster. Then repeat it to yourself until it feels believable. So, for example, if you're stuck in traffic and your negative thought is 'I'm never going to get there on time', stop it and exchange it for 'I always arrive relaxed and in perfect time'. Act as if it's true. Repeat it aloud if you like, making it enjoyable. Go on, don't worry about the person in the car next to you who thinks you're nuts. I bet your journey will ease up and obstacles will magically disappear.

A delegate on a course I was facilitating decided to try this with her boss. Up until that point they'd shared a very difficult working relationship but after a few weeks of modifying her behaviour towards him and pretending that he really liked her, she was amazed to find that he started to treat her differently. A few months later she was promoted, on his recommendation.

Blaming others for our problems is how we give away our power. Having once been in an abusive relationship with a 'dry alcoholic', I fully understand how having a victim mentality can only attract abusers and the quicker we can take responsibility for everything in our world, the faster we can change it. In this situation, sometimes the most loving thing to do (for both parties) is to leave and find a safe place to heal. As you really get to work on loving yourself, the abusive relationship will either change or will lose its hold on you.

Start seeing your partner as your best teacher and make your decisions from a place of love, not fear.

Accept that whatever annoys you about them is really just a part of you that you're rejecting. Go deeper and try to look behind the mask when dealing with others. Everyone is struggling with their pain.

Looking back I can now see that every situation I have been in has been necessary for my growth. It's all-perfect, though at the time I kicked right back. If you'd told me then that a difficult relationship was going to teach me things about myself I wasn't prepared to face at the time, or that my health challenges would spur me on to write this book, I would have given you a very choice response!

Your most important relationship

In a society where falling in love is seen as an achievement, it's easy to feel pressured into having a 'significant other' before we're entitled to declare we're complete. The proliferation of dating clubs, online matchmaking services, singles events, books and courses about attracting your soulmate hints at our obsession with coupledom.

Yet divorce rates are still climbing, prenuptial agreements are commonplace and couples counselling is a booming industry. What is really going on?

It can sometimes be a worthwhile exercise to examine our motives for wanting to be in a relationship. Escapism and attachment are two of the most common reasons. Perhaps we don't want to face ourselves and want to hide behind or attach ourselves to another person. Both are bound to end in disillusionment – with us and the other person – because they are based on insecurity and illusion. If we think we need another, we're saying we're not complete on our own and setting ourselves up for loss, fear and a lack of freedom. And unless we're free to make our own choices we can't be happy.

The tough fact is that until you're completely comfortable in your relationship with yourself, authentic contentment with another will elude you. We can only find true happiness when we relinquish our dependencies and accept our completeness. Paradoxically, only then are we likely to attract people that naturally resonate and connect with us.

Changing your story

Our relationships with people, places, objects and events are all about the stories we tell ourselves. We construct a reality based on our beliefs and because we're projecting that perceived reality onto a situation, we're likely to get the results we expect (thoughts create our reality, remember?), which only goes to reinforce those beliefs as true – according to us. And so the circle is perpetuated. Others will have different experiences of the same event or person, depending on their 'filter.' In the words of Charles Lamb: 'We see the world not as it is, but as we are'.

This principle was made very obvious to me during a trip to Edinburgh with my husband. We both needed to journey to different meetings in the same city, which involved travelling by car, on foot and by train, arriving at roughly the same time.

When the alarm clock went off that morning, I stopped myself getting up and spent a few lovely minutes playing out the forthcoming day in my head. I imagined arriving in good time, relaxed and prepared for my meeting. I saw the meeting going well with some positive outcomes and an enjoyable, relaxed return journey.

Seth meanwhile leapt out of bed, nervously eyed the alarm clock and crashed his way out of the bedroom, grabbing his clothes as he went.

After breakfast, we got into the car together. 'Come on, come on, we're going to miss the train.' I couldn't understand what all the fuss was about; we had more than enough time to comfortably reach the station and park the car. Seth drove down the driveway like a madman, cursing everything under his breath. Usually you might come across a couple of pheasants, a farmer, one or two cars and a handful of school kids on the five-minute journey to the station. This particular morning however, we had to pull over for a cavalcade of cars, a herd of cows, a busload of school kids and a tractor! It took 15 minutes to get to the station.

As we approached the usually empty car park, Seth was bemoaning the fact that we'd never find a space. Sure enough, the car park was full. 'Damn, now we'll never get a seat on the train!' he exploded, as we parked down the road and ran to the platform.

By then I was envisaging two adjoining seats in the third carriage and calmly made my way toward it. Seth was already beating his way toward the second carriage, along with what seemed like most of the local population.

I found our two seats, settled into one, put my briefcase on the other and waited for the whirlwind to arrive. A few minutes later he burst through the door looking very perplexed.

Although way too proud to ask how I'd got two seats on a crowded train, I knew he was intrigued. Some time later I mentioned that I would need to stop at the bank en route to the next station. 'Oh you won't have time to do that. We'll miss the train to Edinburgh and then I'll never make my meeting.'

By this time I'd had enough and pointed out to him that not only was he annoying me, he was also negatively preconditioning his reality. To give him his due, if something's staring him in the face my husband will graciously accept it and our journey continued with no further hiccups. We even managed to have a leisurely walk to our next train, stopped at the bank and arrived in Edinburgh relaxed and happy.

This is in no way meant to absolve me from the crime of negative thinking. I catch myself doing it all the time. It's just an example of a day when I was more conscious than usual. I'm sure you can think of countless examples of similar stories in your life, too.

The truth is, you are the only person in control of your mind, which makes you the storyteller. If you continually write yourself into stories of doom and gloom, frightening yourself with perceptions of what could happen or what might have been, you're much more likely to come to a sticky end. If, however, you take a seat firmly in the centre of your mind and create a fairytale, **that** will be your reality. It is another case of 'change your words, change your world'.

7

ATTRACTING PROSPERITY

'Diligence is the mother of
good fortune.'

Benjamin Disraeli

There are two words in economic parlance, which effectively sum up the secret of financial prosperity: interest and appreciation. If we can foster an interest in acquiring wealth and cultivate an attitude of abundance by appreciation of what we already possess, we're halfway to being better off. Sounds too simple? I'm not rich yet but I do know this works because I've tried it.

Having been virtually bankrupt and known the terror of not having enough incomings to meet the outgoings, when I started the process of changing my financial reality it felt like I was trying to skate uphill with somebody at the top throwing boulders at me. Every time I thought I was making progress, something would come along to flummox me and back down the slippery slope I would go. It literally took me years to shake off my ingrained poverty mentality.

We've all met people who are outwardly successful yet never feel they have enough. They rarely if ever stop to enjoy the fruits of their labours, ploughing on until they experience a heart attack or other life-threatening event. They have the interest in wealth but lack the appreciation of themselves and what they have earned. Their lack of self-worth spurs them onto exhausting efforts of accumulation until eventually their bodies give up.

Conversely there are people who attract money easily, yet are spendthrifts. They certainly appreciate having money but don't have the interest in pursuing or hanging onto it, knowing they will always be able to attract more. Although this might seem like a healthier attitude on the surface, most of the people I've known who are like this drift from one experience to another with a vague sense of dissatisfaction.

Our parents or the adults who raised us lay the basic building blocks of our belief system surrounding prosperity. It's a fascinating exercise to take a large sheet of paper and spend a bit of time listing all the things you learned about money while you were growing up. These can be things you overheard, events you witnessed or just opinions that were taken for granted by your family, for example 'money doesn't grow on trees'. Do try it, it's quite startling when you unearth a belief you've inherited, which may be stopping you from attracting the prosperity you deserve. When I completed this exercise, I was surprised to discover that my fundamental belief that money would only come to me if I worked hard at a 'proper job' was preventing me from succeeding in my chosen field of complementary health. I've now made the necessary adjustments and find it much easier to assign an appropriate value to my time and expertise.

Appreciate your true value

One of the golden nuggets I discovered during my excursions up and down the slippery ice slope was that it's vital to dissociate your financial status from your sense of self-worth. If you look at your bank balance and it's in the red you are *not* a bad person and providing you are taking the necessary steps to attract money, it is *not* a permanent state!

The other trick is to act as if money is not an issue. I don't mean giving fraudulent information or lording around like a millionaire, bending your credit cards at will – tempting though that might be! The assurance I mean is an inner conviction that the universe will provide for you. It starts with a true appreciation of what you do have and progresses to using affirmations for where you want to be financially.

One affirmation, which I use regularly, is 'wealth comes to me from unexpected sources'. Since I started using this every day I've received a surprise tax rebate, an unprompted refund from my electricity supplier and lots of extra paid work from opportunities that presented themselves to me seemingly out of the blue. People have even been repaying small loans that I'd long ago forgotten about and I regularly win prizes in raffles. Exercise a bit of caution though – you do have to be exact. Money from regular sources, such as my salary, started going awry until I added in 'expected and unexpected sources' to my affirmation!

Another time I affirmed for 'abundance in all things' – that week life got pretty busy. My workload doubled so there was paperwork everywhere and the phone rang almost constantly. The dog experienced a phantom pregnancy, throwing us all into a mild panic. The rain fell so heavily that it blocked all the drains. And most of my friends and family decided to visit at the same time, so we had a surplus of food, which I stored in the larder ... and consequently swelled the mouse population to record numbers! So be careful what you wish for!

Accept abundance into your life

What you focus on appreciates. What you appreciate increases in value because where attention goes, energy flows. This is why if you're experiencing financial difficulties, it makes sense to stop worrying about your bills or lack of money. Worrying is pointless. I used to think this was just something your granny said to calm you down, but actually in a metaphysical sense it really adds up. When we worry we are actually focusing on what we don't want to happen. And if our thoughts produce our reality, that's exactly what we are going to create. So switch your attention from what you don't want to happen – this might feel like reining in wild horses – and put all your attention on your desired outcome. If we can positively redirect even a fraction of the energy we usually spend on worrying, just think how powerful our new manifestations will be.

My business mentor uses a handy reminder to prompt her sense of abundance and make sure her finances stay fluid – she keeps a bundle of napkins on show at home, which look like very realistic £50 notes! She regularly entertains friends and dinner guests and when they first see the piles of 'money' placed strategically around the house, their initial reactions to her *laissez-faire* attitude to cash vary considerably. Some are horrified that she can be so ostentatious. Others think she's naïve or careless. Very few seem to be impressed by her obvious abundance. When they find out the truth, of course, most people recognize the pure genius of such a gesture and many have gone on to devise prompts of their own. But it's an interesting example of our ingrained attitudes toward prosperity.

Our status in life is closely linked with what we think we deserve. If we attract a positive experience and don't feel worthy of it, then we will often sabotage our enjoyment of it. I have known people from all backgrounds, rich and poor, yet the universal truth that keeps people where they are within the spectrum (unless they decide to change), is whether they hold a framework of poverty or prosperity consciousness.

Regardless of how much money you have, if you're feeling trapped or that there's no alternative, you're suffering from poverty consciousness. Money, like emotion, is an energy that needs to flow. People who have successfully developed prosperity consciousness know that there is only one source of abundance – the Universe. It's a huge storehouse of wealth and the only thing that blocks our access to it is our limiting beliefs. Research shows that even people who win the lottery are likely to return to their original financial state (or worse) within just two years unless they change their consciousness!

What's your worth?

Here's an interesting exercise to try. Stand in front of a full-length mirror and ask yourself how much you deserve to earn as an annual salary. Start at the minimum acceptable wage and keep doubling it, saying 'I deserve to earn (insert figure) every year' and watching your body language the whole time. You'll quickly reach a figure that makes you uncomfortable. You might find you can't meet your own gaze when you speak the words, or you may experience some discomfort within your body, which makes you want to move or turn away. Once you reach this figure, gradually decrease it until you feel comfortable again. This is your money comfort level and I would bet my bottom dollar that if you look back over your finances for the past few years, this is how much you've 'allowed' yourself to earn!

The good news is we can change this figure – if we're prepared to go through the comfort barrier. Suspend your disbelief for a little while and stop trying to calculate how you're going to increase your earnings. That's not for you to worry about. If you can work on changing the beliefs about what you deserve and start believing them, the universe will figure out the details. The trick is to see your money comfort level as a thermostat. Just like the heating or air-conditioning system in your home or workplace, every room will have a thermostat, which allows you to adjust the temperature. When the room reaches the required temperature, the thermostat switches off the supply of warm or cool air. Your money thermostat works the same way, regulating your income.

So take a deep breath and look yourself in the eye. With all your confidence, declare that you deserve to earn an amount that's 10 per cent more than you earned last year. If that feels OK, increase it to 20 per cent and so on until you reach a new comfort level. Stop when you want to, but make a commitment to do this every day until you feel you've reset your thermostat to a higher level. Each time you do this it gets easier and you should find you become more comfortable with your deservability. Then watch your finances reorganize themselves as if by magic!

Affirmations such as 'I have plenty of money', or 'I am always able to pay my bills', are great to use if you're feeling insecure about money. Clearing out your cupboards and wardrobes is another way to demonstrate to the universe that you're ready for new things and experiences to flow into your life.

Prosperity, of course, is not just limited to your financial situation. True richness is experienced when we feel loved and can lead a fulfilled life. The following gave me the courage and inspiration to take my first steps on the road to the life of my dreams.

Practise saying 'yes' to the universe

You can seek guidance all you like but unless you act on it, it doesn't have the power to change your world. Have you ever been presented with an opportunity and automatically ruled it out because you thought you'd never be able to do it? I would regularly ask the universe to help me attract clients to my workshops. I'd remember to do my affirmations, prepare the material, book the venue and send out the emails but whenever someone invited me to give a talk I would turn them down flat, all because of a belief that I was no good at public speaking. Refusal became so unconscious that I couldn't even remember being asked, and remained puzzled that I wasn't getting my message out, yet there must have been dozens of invitations.

Thankfully a friend pointed this out to me and I started to say 'yes' to the universe. Even though I was terrified initially, I learned the importance of 'fake it 'til you make it', and now I can confidently give a talk without notes.

The buzz of achievement is really quite addictive. Please just try it. Start by saying 'yes' to one thing this week that you wouldn't usually consider. Your horizons will extend in surprising directions. The universe is your infinite store of abundance – it's just waiting for you to start placing orders!

Practise saying 'no' to things you don't want

We all have obligations to family, friends, work, our homes and interests. And as we squeeze more and more into our lives, the joy leaks out and we have to create a legitimate excuse for not doing something. Hence we get sick. The world won't topple off its axis if you take a holiday, miss a parents' meeting, or don't mow the lawn every weekend. Practise saying 'no' to a few of these demands on your time, and, providing you are polite but firm, people will start respecting your boundaries. Avoid negative people who drain your energy.

This also goes for negative thinking. The only person who's in control in your mind is you. If you tune into your mental chatter it can be like a running commentary on your life and everyone you meet. Your belief systems are played out on this continuous loop and it's easy to think someone else is running the show. We've become so accustomed to this background chatter that most of the time it runs unchecked. Get conscious and establish who is boss in there! If you uncover a limiting belief such as 'there's not enough money', thank it for sharing and then replace it with a supportive affirmation. If you have trouble banishing the negatives, bring to mind experiences that make you feel good, remembering that each time you do this you will be forging new neural pathways in your brain. Only you can do this. There is no one else inside your head!

Never give begrudgingly – if you're clear you don't want to do something, don't do it. Stay conscious of your motives, your choices. You don't always have to make instant decisions and there are always choices in how you respond to requests.

Expect success!

Positive things begin to happen when we start expecting them to manifest. Here's an experiment – play with it, it's fun: for the next week just pretend that you believe life is conspiring with, not against you. Imagine that everybody is acting in your best interests and that everything will work out for the best. Look for every silver lining, compliment and bless as many people as you can (even if it feels false to begin with), turn every problem into an opportunity and affirm that you deserve only the best. Start trusting in love and life and your flow of good is bound to increase!

Prosperity is not limited to having enough money. Take a few moments to think back to moments when you felt successful. Remember that feeling of expansion in your chest, that sense that anything was possible. It's unlikely the feeling was directly linked to money. Often it's achievements that breed success and self-worth. Perhaps you managed to give up smoking or kept your cool under pressure; maybe you transformed a limiting belief or released a childhood fear. Falling in love, passing a test, doing something that makes your heart sing or being recognized for a unique talent are all definitions of prosperity.

Too often we fall into the trap of thinking we need to 'have' something to 'be' something (for example we need to have money to be happy) when in fact it's the other way round. Success follows intention and the feeling has to come first. Only by *feeling* prosperous can we *be* prosperous. It really is that simple. So if you believe that having money will allow you to feel more secure, cultivate that sense of security first and you will be putting yourself directly in the flow of money.

The first step in effecting any change in your circumstances is to accept responsibility for them. Look to see how your thoughts may have created your situation. Are you holding onto an outdated belief or fear that because you made a mistake in the past you are likely to fail again? Do you feel that good only ever happens to other people? Has your family belief system programmed you to believe that the only way money will come to you is by being dishonest or winning the lottery? All these thoughts will keep you locked in the past or yearning for the future and that is not where the magic happens.

Being entirely present and keeping your heart and mind open to new possibilities is the way forward.

Don't beat yourself up for whatever conditions you've created in the past, this is a new moment! You can begin creating prosperity consciousness anytime you want to. Ask for help from friends, loved ones and the universe as you make the transition to a new way of looking at the world. The more support you have, the easier it will be for you to let go of limiting beliefs.

Once you're clear about which thoughts and beliefs may be keeping you from your highest good you can get to work on changing them. Create some positive affirmations, which sum up how you'd like to be demonstrating prosperity in your life, for example: 'I am rich beyond my wildest dreams!' If that's too big an initial step, start with 'I am a magnet for money.' Keep your affirmations as unlimited as possible because you are unlikely to have thought of every way the universe can bring you your heart's desire.

Manifest your dreams

The absolute keys to successful manifestation are:

1. **Focus on the feeling** you want to generate. Each time you think about money or prosperity, bring to mind an experience in the past where you felt successful. If it's peace of mind you want, start noticing everything

in your day-to-day life that brings you peace of mind. Perhaps it comes from sinking into a nice warm bath, knowing your kids are safely tucked up in bed. Or maybe it's that sense of offloading a burden when you chat to a close friend. Meditate on that feeling of security and stop to enjoy it whenever it crosses your path.

2. **Be very clear on how you want to feel** without being at all attached to how that will come into being. Remember that if you bring any negative emotion into this process, such as feeling you can't live without something, you will actually push away what you're trying to attract.

3. **Appreciate every single step** you take toward achieving that feeling. So if you're focusing on creating abundance in your life and you find a coin in your pocket, express your gratitude and celebrate.

Another way to increase the flow of good things into your life is to realize that there is plenty for everyone. Every time you are grateful for any money and blessings and send them out with joy and love, imagine your money bringing pleasure to whoever receives it. This act of generosity accompanied by your newfound feelings of security will open up the universal channels of abundance.

8

Nourishing Body, Mind and Spirit

'True happiness involves the full use
of one's power and talents.'

John W Gardner

So often we confuse 'self-love' with egotism, when actually it's impossible to fully love others unless we have a healthy respect for ourselves.

In Scotland especially, I have noticed that people find this concept particularly difficult. Having been brought up with the instruction to never 'blow your own trumpet' in case you get 'too big for your boots' many people shy away from any kind of praise or celebration of themselves and their achievements. But this is not about being bigheaded or arrogant. It's about value. You can't truly love someone else until you love and accept yourself. And they can't really love you until you let them!

So love and accept yourself exactly as you are. Not how you imagine you'll be when you've lost weight or had your teeth fixed or cleared your debts – *exactly as you are*, warts and all. I think this is probably the most difficult invocation of all, yet if we can truly master it we also fall in love with all of life, giving us access to boundless joy and energy. In this state of grace, 'problems' magically dissolve and life becomes an intriguing adventure.

Stop all criticism

That means of others **and yourself**. Criticism breaks

down the inner spirit, whereas praise builds it up. You might find this means you can't join in with some conversations, so accustomed have we become to focusing on the negative in life. That's fine; just start one of your own. People will begin seeking you out when they realize how inspiring you are to be around!

I'm not suggesting that we deny the unpleasant truths in our world and ourselves; there's no need to be a Polyanna. If we can accept everything, 'good' and 'bad', but choose to focus on the positive, it's easier to keep a balanced perspective. Criticism and negativity are insidious and can creep into our lives without us noticing them, so it's important to manage our thoughts and consciously choose our actions. I find it helps to read positive affirmations or work on my gratitude journal before going to bed and I make a point of not watching the news before sleep.

Practise self-nurture

Run a scented bath, treat yourself to a massage, buy yourself that album, book a holiday, spend time with friends ... whatever floats your boat! If we include ourselves among those we love, our lives will be enriched. Try to treat yourself at least once a week or once a day if possible. It doesn't always have to be a big gift – sometimes the little things bring the most pleasure.

Love is always an 'inside job'. We are conditioned to think from an early age that there is a handsome prince or beautiful princess out there for us that will make our lives perfect, however, this is not the full story. If we spend our time waiting for our 'other half' to come along we're stalling our development. Children especially need to be encouraged to recognize their strengths and develop a strong sense of self-worth. You are a unique and wonderful human being in your own right and it's far better to foster love for yourself than wait for someone else to complete you. By self-love I don't mean vanity or arrogance – they are actually forms of low self-worth – but a deep respect and gratitude for who you are.

Praise, praise, praise the divinity within. Use positive affirmations such as 'I deserve the very best in life' to claim your magnificence and watch your daily existence transform. Change can be daunting and, as you improve your own experience, everyone else in your world is likely to feel the shift because we're all one. This can sometimes create uneasiness and fear, particularly in your closest relationships, so it's a good idea to surround yourself with positive friends and thoughts that nurture you and make you feel good. Perhaps you could create a happy book and start collecting things – stories, poems and letters – that bring you joy. Also note down your favourite things to do; your treasured films, songs, books, people, memories, tastes, smells, activities, etc. Just continue to take little steps and celebrate every single one of your successes.

One step at a time

My coaching clients usually come to me when they've reached the end of their tether so their lives are often not flowing on more than one level. When they start looking within and working on loving themselves there is a tendency to take everything on board at once, which inevitably leads to overload and disillusionment. While it's good to see the whole picture, taking a gentler approach is a much more loving and sustainable way to treat yourself so I always encourage people to concentrate on one step at a time. Whether that's health, relationships, money, success or life purpose, choose the one that resonates the most with your heart and work with that issue first. There's plenty of time to untangle the others – patience and compassion will help you along the road.

Some clients experience a 'healing crisis', which is a very dramatic name for a detox. As old habits and thought patterns are released, particularly if you're working on health issues, you might feel a bit worse before you start to feel better. This is nothing to be alarmed about – it's just the body's way of naturally rebalancing itself and if you keep your focus on your positive affirmations this stage will pass quickly. It's another good reason to be extra kind to yourself.

Liberate yourself from stress

Stress is a well-worn word in our rushed world. One definition of stress is having to make too many decisions in too short a space of time. It shows up in our lives as pain or discomfort, an obvious signal to ourselves that something needs to change. Yet we've become so accustomed – some would even say addicted – to stress in our lives that we imagine we'd find it difficult to function without it. Stress has become the constant companion rather than the messenger it was meant to be.

What we're really 'addicted' to is the hit of the stimulating chemicals cortisol and adrenaline as they enter our bloodstream, which makes us feel more alive for a brief moment. But there are other less painful ways of enlivening our experience by deepening the moment.

Regular meditation each day will help you physically and mentally slow down by returning your mind to the theta state. Remember how as a kid every day seemed to stretch for miles? And a year seemed like forever! The reason for this is that your attention wasn't scattered. You weren't living part in the past, part in the future, but instead brought your whole energetic being into the present. This is true mindfulness; the ability to devote yourself entirely to one activity, and it will enrich your life beyond measure. If you can slow down your speech as well and take the trouble to really listen to and engage with the other person you'll find that communication becomes a feast of the senses; a much deeper, more enjoyable experience.

Words can become as melodic as music when we savour them and give them our full attention. Hold your thoughts in your mouth before you speak them and soak them in the honey of your loving intent – conversations will be transformed and you'll be bringing a little more peace into the world.

Look after your body

Your body is a wonderful vehicle for expressing who you are and it's perfectly capable of healing itself if you create the necessary conditions for good health. If you nourish it with health-giving food and drink, rest when you need to, cultivate a happy, peaceful mind and exercise daily – preferably outdoors – your body will respond in appreciation.

I encourage my clients to drink lots of water. As well as the physical cleansing it brings, it's also great for energetic flushing. If you've been working on emotional issues it can help you let go of any residue and flush them out of your system. I'm not quite sure how this works, but it does.

Nutrition is another important building block of good health and there are plenty of paths to explore until you find the right eating plan for you. One size definitely does not fit all and I'd be wary of diets that make this claim. The only diets that truly work are abstaining from negative thoughts about yourself and others and really working on loving yourself. Some extra bonuses of this approach are that as you accept yourself exactly as you are and your weight starts to normalize, any addictions you're holding onto will naturally drop away and you'll probably start to look younger, too.

Bodies love to move and if you watch a child you'll notice they naturally find it difficult to keep still. As we grow older we tend to replace this movement with much more restricted and 'acceptable' behaviour. I honestly believe this is detrimental to our health and can contribute to stagnant emotions. If you can, find a form of exercise that allows you freedom of expression. If gyms bore you, get out into nature and walk among the trees and flowers wherever you can – I guarantee you'll feel uplifted. Swim, dance, climb, run, skip, cycle, ride a horse or turn cartwheels – whatever you choose make sure it causes your lungs to fill and your heart to sing. The benefits will be physical, mental and spiritual and you're much more likely to make time for it in your schedule if it doesn't feel like a chore.

Resting is just as important as exercise and deep breathing practices such as meditation and yoga can really help you relax. If you have trouble sleeping, imagine yourself as full of liquid, which drains out of your body with every breath.

Another effective technique is unhooking your energetic connections before you drop off to sleep. See everything you're 'hooked up' on – unresolved conflicts, worries or tensions – as a large S-shaped meat hook and picture yourself unhooking them one by one and dropping them down and out through your feet. Before you get to the last hook you'll be fast asleep.

Express your emotions

We live in a society where it's rarely OK to express what we're feeling. Boys don't cry, the stiff upper lip, nice girls don't sleep around, survival of the fittest, the 'war' on a) terror, b) drugs, c) germs, d) crime, e) you name it – all these stories have only served to keep us emotionally repressed. By portraying some emotions as weak and glorifying more aggressive feelings, we have created a few acceptable and therefore very pressurized 'channels' of emotion, such as war, sport, competition and celebrity. In England we witnessed an acute national crisis when Princess Diana was killed in a car crash. Tragic though the story was, the outpouring of grief was completely out of proportion with the event itself, and is still intensely felt by some, even though ten years has elapsed. I can only surmise that because a celebrity was involved, such public grief is deemed 'OK'. My beloved grandmother died the same week; even her funeral became a eulogy to Princess Diana. I still miss her terribly, yet if I had continued to grieve publicly for her loss to the same extent, I would probably have been prescribed some strong medication by now.

We are not born repressed. If you watch a child for a day, you'll see them move effortlessly through a whole range of emotions, and they're certainly not afraid to express them. As we grow we learn to adopt masks or 'coping strategies', which we present to the world. We are taught to 'deal with it.' But rather than dealing with our feelings properly we often stuff them deep inside ourselves where they continue to create havoc for years to come.

Re-directing this energy is crucial for positive health. If it's not appropriate for you to scream, cry, kick and yell in the moment, set aside some private time with your favourite loud rock music, a pillow or a mattress. Lock the door and really go for it! Throw a tantrum if you like. No one is watching or judging you and I guarantee you'll feel much better (and fitter) after pounding out your frustrations for ten minutes. Tears need to be expressed, so if during this process you start to recall an upsetting experience, don't be afraid to cry and howl until you feel empty. Think of it like riding a wave on the river of life.

As soon as you become aware of an emotion and really feel it, it loses its intensity. How often have you felt something really strongly and been in the middle of expressing it only to find that you don't feel it's true anymore? This is because e-motions are energy in motion. They need to move. If we store them away inside, the energy they carry becomes destructive. If we can learn to really feel them and let them out safely, the energy we release can be used for more constructive outcomes – like manifesting your ideal life.

Nourish your spirit

In the rush of our daily existence it is often our spirits that get neglected, as we split our time between past and future. Forgetting we are spiritual beings first and foremost, we set about serving the body and mind and act surprised when our attention is brought back to the present – usually with a jolt such as illness or accidents.

Spending just a fraction of your time 'hanging out' in the silence with your spiritual self each day will do wonders for your equilibrium. Even five minutes' meditation in the morning and five more before you go to bed will start to make a difference in your life, and you'll feel more balanced, calm and peaceful as you practice. A lovely affirmation or mantra to use is:

'I am a whole person releasing my full potential.'

If you like to sing, sing. If you prefer to pray, pray. Write some poetry, dance in the rain, go on a picnic, paint a picture, bake a cake, wrap yourself up in a duvet and watch cartoons all day. Do something that makes your soul smile as often as possible. You are a child of the universe – act like one!

Play with your inner child

It's tempting to believe that as we grow up we leave our 'inner child' behind but I think that causes us to miss out on an opportunity. To live truly in the moment, to dance as though we're not being watched, love as though we've never been hurt before, sing as though no one can hear us and live as though heaven is on Earth means to exist in the present, much like a child. 'Impossible!' you may say. 'I have work to do, bills to pay, things to plan.' That may be true but there are also moments in every day when we can be mindfully present and these are the moments we should seize.

When was the last time you spoke to 'little you'? How many years ago did you give into the urge to play at something, just because you felt like it? This is your soul speaking to you. When we take the time to go within and listen, that little child may be clamouring for our attention. Or they may have given up trying to communicate with us and be sitting in sullen silence.

Wherever he or she is now, I urge you to make contact. If you can only set aside five minutes, take the time to talk to her, get to know him better. They'll soon let you know how you can make them happy. Reassure them that they are safe and loved, that's all your inner child needs.

An exercise that really helps this reconnection is drawing a picture of yourself as a child, using your non-dominant hand. Use colour if you can – colours can tell you a lot about your emotions. When you look at the picture notice how it makes you feel – are they happy or sad, frustrated or carefree? If there are areas of fuzziness, denseness or odd angles in your drawing, how does this relate to your feelings about different parts of your body? This might feel really silly at first but it's surprising how it can put you back in touch with feelings and dreams you'd stuffed away inside your adult self.

Once you've re-established a connection with your little girl or boy, ask him or her to travel with you – perhaps there's a space big enough in your heart. You'll be surprised and delighted when life becomes more spontaneous and fun and perhaps you'll choose to follow your heart sometimes instead of your head. Maybe you'll even dust off some of those old dreams.

9

SERVING THE WORLD

'You must be the change you wish
to see in the world.'

Mohandas Gandhi

We are living in exciting and turbulent times. I believe we are on the threshold of a spiritual evolution, which will transform life on this planet. Technological progress is accelerating beyond the understanding of most people, global communication networks have webbed nations together in an unprecedented fashion and children are being born with syndromes we have never had names for before. Depending on your viewpoint all this change can be interpreted as evolution or apocalypse – you will decide.

Whatever your standpoint, this transition presents an opportunity to become the highest versions of ourselves. It calls on all our masculine and feminine qualities to bring this world back into balance.

We are born into this world as messengers of love. If you've ever gazed into a young baby's eyes you will have seen reflected infinite pools of love and truth. Fears are learned; love is natural. As small babies we know we're all one – the knowledge that we are separate beings from our mothers takes months to develop and we act all surprised when we discover we have a body of our own.

Our mission on this planet is to regroup, to remember that original wisdom, to love everyone including ourselves. As Marianne Williamson says 'nothing liberates our greatness like the desire to help, the desire to serve.'

Serving others is actually acting in your best interests. If you're living a lot of your time with others' wellbeing at heart, you'll find you feel great about yourself, whereas if you spend too much time in a me-centred universe you'll tend to be frustrated and intolerant. This is because giving causes us to notice that we have something to give. So when we give with love we can't help but feel that love on its way out, which means we experience giving as receiving and know ourselves as being 'love'. And if we're open to receiving love from others we're giving them an opportunity to demonstrate who they really are too. Too often we stop ourselves from giving because of a belief in scarcity. We worry that there is not enough love to go around. In reality there's a limitless supply because love is all there is.

In his poetic book *The Gentle Art of Blessing* Pierre Pradervand speaks of the importance of giving silent blessings. To bless means to expect and wish unconditionally for the good of others, to see past their limitations to the true spiritual being beyond. His inspirational book gives countless examples of these blessings in action, revealing their transformative power in the most everyday situations.

I have always been taught to bless every person and situation that crosses my path, however challenging, and it's encouraging to see people's troubles lift when you consciously remember to do this. Sometimes blessings are the only tools available to us.

Altered perceptions

How do you deal with big changes in your world? Are you traumatized, incredulous, in denial, excited? When troubles befall you, do you dwell on your misfortune or extract the teaching and turn your thoughts to more positive outcomes? Even if a catastrophic event happens thousands of miles away, the effect will be a personal one, felt and dealt with within our own consciousness.

Our beliefs are built on our perceptions and our actions on our beliefs, which is why there can be so many different responses to a single incident. Greater circumstances are largely beyond our control and the only things we have true authority over are our perceptions, which on the surface might seem like bad news. However, if we can master our perceptions and turn reaction into response, we will gain resilience and be of much more service to the world.

Managing our perceptions and 'choosing' our reality takes dedication and daily practice. We tend to construct our reality and think thereafter 'this is how life works'. These mental models are inbuilt for survival, and can work very well when we instinctively run from a predator, but it's vital to examine them regularly to make sure they are still useful.

The difference between 'ordinary' people like us and 'enlightened' masters is that masters continually choose the same response, regardless of the situation. In the face of peace and instability they maintain their inner poise. This requires a complete reversal of what is probably for most of us a lifelong habit – needing something outside ourselves to provide comfort or happiness.

We have been schooled to believe that we need something or someone else to make us feel complete. Cigarettes, alcohol, drugs, acceptance, clothes, 'the latest' anything, a soul mate, fame and fortune ... you fill in the blanks. We bounce from one experience to the next, looking for the sticking plaster that will fix us. In truth though, any thing, idea or person that promotes dependency is a misguided belief as we already have whatever we're looking for.

True happiness and contentment is nothing more than a decision. A very important decision, but a decision nonetheless – and one we'll have the opportunity to make every second of every day. We can steer our own ship through life and don't need to buy into other people's versions of reality. Cultivating an attitude of non-judgement, peace and clarity and choosing to respond to every situation with thoughts, words and actions of love are the best gift you can give and the only way to truly change the world.

Any true manifestation in the world requires a shift in consciousness, an insight into the true nature of reality. Japanese haiku poetry is an example of this; it was once explained to me that despite its often-rigorous structure (usually 17 syllables divided into three lines of five, seven and five), the true haiku always leaves room for the transformative breath of God.

Each of us has the ability to change consciousness through our behaviour. I'm sure you've noticed the effect on others when someone walks into a room in a grumpy or gloomy mood. In my management training I once learned that a positive person is only likely to influence two others, whereas a negative person can influence up to nine!

To be a positive influence and generate a higher quality of energy, you'll need to straddle a bit of a paradox – raising your consciousness while staying grounded. Retreating from the world may seem like a tempting option when chaos reigns, but interacting with others is the fastest route to enlightenment. Only in relationship to others can we truly see ourselves and work out our 'stuff'. If we can deal with others in the 'right' way, projecting the energy of love, we can resolve our own issues and free up our energy to vibrate on a higher level.

Empathy versus sympathy

Another apparent contradiction is empathy versus sympathy. If we identify or sympathize with another person's predicament we suffer alongside them, which limits the amount of help we can give. Empathy allows us to understand another's feelings without taking them into ourselves, leaving us free to offer stability and positive encouragement for the other person.

Our willingness to help others often sees us leaping in to 'rescue' them. A tragic local story brought home the futility of this for me at the end of last year. As you might know, rain is an almost permanent feature of the west of Scotland, particularly in the winter months and last year was no exception. As a result, the River Garnock burst its banks and a young family's pet dogs were swept away in the torrent while they were out for a walk. The father and mother were both drowned trying to rescue the dogs, leaving their seven-month old baby daughter without any parents. How different the ending might have been if one of the adults had stayed on the bank.

Often the most effective tool we have is our ability to send positive thoughts or prayers toward a person or situation. Our charity is linked to a forum, which has been running consistently for ten years. Every Friday we send messages of hope and support to our friends around the world. If someone is in need of help their name is put forward and we all hold them in a positive light. Over the years there have been some miraculous healings, with tumours disappearing, conditions being reversed and rapid recoveries taking place. Love heals.

I never cease to be amazed by our collective muscle. When we choose to unite behind a common cause or perceived injustice, our thoughts, words and actions are a force to be reckoned with. Of course under the surface we are all united but most of the time we have lost our awareness of that oneness, believing instead in separation. Despite this fragmentation our souls crave harmony and having been lucky enough to experience spiritual unity with large groups of people, I think it's the 'fix' we've all been looking for!

Shortly before finishing this book I was on the receiving end of some good luck. A video produced by my web copywriting company 'went viral' on the social networks. It wasn't planned – I was actually on holiday when it happened – and the response took us all by surprise. Watching its popularity climb into millions of views and receiving many thousands of heartfelt responses was an exhilarating and slightly surreal experience.

Within weeks we had offers of work and collaboration from across the globe. People I'd never met were telling me they loved – or hated – me, and multi-national companies were phoning day and night. It was as if every shade of humanity had shown up on my doorstep demanding to be heard. What really blew me away was the thought that prior to the internet such a phenomena would never have been possible. Within a month we had received several thousand emails and had enough business to keep us going for several years!

As if that wasn't surprising enough, the month before it happened I had virtually decided to turn my attention away from the business in favour of my more 'spiritual' and charitable work in the field of health and wellbeing. I couldn't see the link between the work I was doing – writing content for websites – and serving the world in a meaningful way.

The video is called *The Power of Words* and had already been in the public domain for over a year before it became popular. We originally created it as an homage to an award-winning film we'd admired – *Historia de un Letrero* by Alonso Alvarez Barreda – and shortened it for the web. When it came to gracing the video with a subtitle I took a moment to meditate and came up with *Change Your Words, Change Your World*, which seemed to sum up what we were offering in terms of web content. We uploaded it to YouTube almost as an afterthought.

During the months when I was deliberating what to do with my web copywriting company, a business mentor I'd been consulting asked what I really wanted to achieve. When she learned that I'd been agonizing over how I could combine my copywriting business with the coaching and healing work, which was really calling me, she advised me to craft a relevant affirmation. She was also the one to point out that my video subtitle perfectly summed up **both** strands of my work and suggested I started taking my own message more seriously!

So for the month before we went on holiday I faithfully wrote out 'I release the need to do work that's not in alignment with my soul' and started to change the way I thought and spoke about my work in the world. Whenever anyone asked me what I did, the response would be 'I help people change their world by changing their words' – it really seemed to catch people's attention!

Since the video went viral the simple truth of this catchphrase seems to have engaged the hearts and minds of a lot more people. Although it has inevitably attracted its share of negative comments, most of the feedback has been extremely positive and uplifting. A world peace project, several book launches, environmental campaigns and a multi-national music festival are just some of the opportunities this success has spawned. Another benefit of the publicity has been the funds raised and interest shown in our charity, Salem Scotland, which will help us to further 'change the world' through our work with carers and young people.

All of this just goes to illustrate how powerful you are. Every single one of us is creating our reality according to our thoughts, words, beliefs and actions. How amazing is that? All you have to do is decide what you are doing (or perhaps more importantly who you are being) for the greater good. The universe will take care of the details.

In conclusion

At the time of writing (end of October 2011), we are seeing some extraordinary events in the world. Large traditional institutions such as banks and media corporations (and even global dictators) are being toppled, and greed and corruption are being 'ousted' on a daily basis. Rather than seeing this as the 'end times' I must admit to being very excited. All this activity suggests we're approaching a tipping point, which will catapult us into a new reality and if enough of us channel our thoughts into positive outcomes we have more of a chance of collectively creating a society based on the only real truths: love, joy and peace.

This evolution will require each and every one of us to assume responsibility for our part in this elaborate play. It calls us to be the best of ourselves, to accept that we are co-creators of the highest order and that our beliefs give rise to our thoughts and words, which birth our actions. Surely this is a comforting thought? We *don't* have to save the planet, eliminate poverty, feed the starving or change the world. At least not on our own! Those thoughts are *way* too big and more often than not will generate mental defeat and lead to a sense of hopelessness and inaction. But if each of us begins by tending our own backyards and changing our own belief systems and ways of interacting and communicating, to reflect peace, joy and love wherever our lives touch upon another person's, the world will naturally change itself.

The potency of your highest thought, the strength of your strongest belief, the balm of your softest word and the truth of your most honourable action can shift everyone's experience of life on this planet. And it's the little kindnesses that matter most.

Don't waste another moment, the world needs you ...

Acknowledgements

Like most authors, I've spent the past few years saying 'I'm working on a book'. In truth, the book has been working on me. So I would like to say a special thanks to all my lovely friends and family at home and abroad for putting up with me and keeping me on track when the going got a little tough – you know who you are and how much you mean to me ☺

I owe an enormous hug of gratitude to David Hamilton who helped keep the dream alive and cheered every step, and to Amy, Michelle, Dan, Jo, Ed and Sandy at Hay House Publishers for their patient and caring professionalism.

The wisdom and encouragement I received from fellow authors Thom Hartmann and Mark Robert Waldman made this book what it is and I'll be eternally grateful for their input.

Thanks also to Luke and Lina Borwick for letting me live in their castle; to the staff at the Rowan Tree Restaurant for giving me a second home; and Alex, Jonny and 'Star' for their enthusiastic book promotion.

ABOUT THE AUTHOR

Andrea Gardner is a writer and online content specialist with more than 10 years' experience of shaping compelling copy for web pages, email campaigns and online features. She started her career in newspaper marketing and features writing before migrating online and establishing Purplefeather in 2003. Clients as diverse as Hilton International, BBC Scotland, Macdonald Hotels and the National Australia Banking Group have reaped the benefits of her optimised copy-crafting and glowing testimonials from New Zealand dentists, Belgian diamond merchants, New York denim designers, Maldivian five-star hotels and Canadian fashion retailers grace her inbox.

Words are her friends. She spends a lot of time alternately loving them, hating them, wrestling and playing with them, all in the name of developing a meaningful relationship. Most of all she enjoys pulling them back into shape when they've lost their way...they often return the favour.

Andrea passionately believes in her motto 'Change Your Words; Change Your World' and retrained as a Heal Your Life workshop leader in 2006, so that she could help more people re-shape their inner dialogues and take back the reins of their lives. She runs regular self-development workshops in the UK and has recently delivered corporate seminars in London, Cairo and Scotland.

www.purplefeather.co.uk

We hope you enjoyed this Hay House book.
If you would like to receive a free catalogue featuring additional
Hay House books and products, or if you would like information
about the Hay Foundation, please contact:

Hay House UK Ltd
292B Kensal Road • London W10 5BE
Tel: (44) 20 8962 1230; Fax: (44) 20 8962 1239
www.hayhouse.co.uk

***

Published and distributed in the United States of America by:
Hay House, Inc. • PO Box 5100 • Carlsbad, CA 92018-5100
Tel: (1) 760 431 7695 or (1) 800 654 5126;
Fax: (1) 760 431 6948 or (1) 800 650 5115
www.hayhouse.com

***

Published and distributed in Australia by:
Hay House Australia Ltd • 18/36 Ralph Street • Alexandria, NSW 2015
Tel: (61) 2 9669 4299, Fax: (61) 2 9669 4144
www.hayhouse.com.au

***

Published and distributed in the Republic of South Africa by:
Hay House SA (Pty) Ltd • PO Box 990 • Witkoppen 2068
Tel/Fax: (27) 11 467 8904
www.hayhouse.co.za

***

Published and distributed in India by:
Hay House Publishers India • Muskaan Complex • Plot No.3
B-2• Vasant Kunj • New Delhi - 110 070
Tel: (91) 11 41761620; Fax: (91) 11 41761630
www.hayhouse.co.in

***

Distributed in Canada by:
Raincoast • 9050 Shaughnessy St • Vancouver, BC V6P 6E5
Tel: (1) 604 323 7100
Fax: (1) 604 323 2600

***

Sign up via the Hay House UK website to receive the Hay House
online newsletter and stay informed about what's going on with your
favourite authors. You'll receive bimonthly announcements
about discounts and offers, special events, product highlights,
free excerpts, giveaways, and more!
www.hayhouse.co.uk

JOIN THE HAY HOUSE FAMILY

As the leading self-help, mind, body and spirit publisher in the UK, we'd like to welcome you to our family so that you can enjoy all the benefits our website has to offer.

 EXTRACTS from a selection of your favourite author titles

 COMPETITIONS, PRIZES & SPECIAL OFFERS Win extracts, money off, downloads and so much more

 LISTEN to a range of radio interviews and our latest audio publications

 CELEBRATE YOUR BIRTHDAY An inspiring gift will be sent your way

 LATEST NEWS Keep up with the latest news from and about our authors

 ATTEND OUR AUTHOR EVENTS Be the first to hear about our author events

 iPHONE APPS Download your favourite app for your iPhone

 HAY HOUSE INFORMATION Ask us anything, all enquiries answered

join us online at **www.hayhouse.co.uk**

 292B Kensal Road, London W10 5BE
T: 020 8962 1230 E: info@hayhouse.co.uk

CPSIA information can be obtained at www.ICGtesting.com
Printed in the USA
BVOW020240041012

302064BV00001B/1/P